Managing Your Academic

Managing Your
Academic Career

Strategies for success

D. Royce Sadler

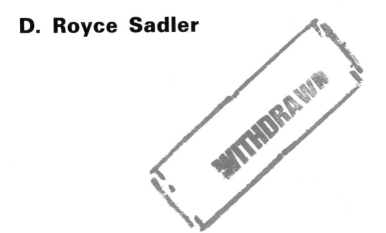

ALLEN & UNWIN

First published in 1999 by
Allen & Unwin
9 Atchison Street, St Leonards NSW 1590 Australia
Phone: (61 2) 8425 0100
Fax: (61 2) 9906 2218
E-mail: frontdesk@allen-unwin.com.au
Web: http://www.allen-unwin.com.au

National Library of Australia
Cataloguing-in-Publication entry:

Sadler, D. Royce (David Royce).
  Managing your academic career: strategies for success.

  Bibliography.
  Includes index.
  ISBN 1 86448 984 7.

  1. College teachers—Employment. 2. College teaching—Vocational
  guidance. I. Title.

378.125023

Set in 11/13 pt Adobe Garamond by DOCUPRO, Sydney
Printed by SRM Production Services Sdn Bhd, Malaysia

10 9 8 7 6 5 4 3 2 1

For Calvin and Josaphine

Contents

Acknowledgments

I have a lot of people to thank. I am grateful to Griffith University for awarding me a period of special research leave. This freed me from teaching and administration so that I could write without hindrance. Thank you Judy Langton for typing the first transcripts from tape. A number of colleagues from a range of disciplines and universities read early versions of some of the chapters and provided valuable feedback that led to material improvement. I refer to Karen Hinett, Mary Keyes, Archie McKay, Janine Collins, Paul Grieve, Rita Di Mascio, Annie McCluskey, Joanna Peters, Parlo Singh, Paul Weeden and Heather Chipuer. None of them, however, is to be held accountable for the final result.

Thanks are also due to the original recipients of many of my memoranda. I am sure none of us saw them as raw material for a book at the time they were written. I thank all the participants in professional development workshops and seminars who asked me tough questions, spoke about their frustrations and dilemmas, or expressed concerns about problematic elements of academic life. I never would have imagined half of these things without you. Ann Crabb, from the publishers Allen & Unwin, provided great support and quick responses to my e-mailed queries. The publishers' reviewers and editors provided valuable insights and suggestions that led to modifications in the final stages of writing. Ashley Sadler and Merideth Sadler, family critics and editors, helped with style and proofreading.

Finally, I am enormously indebted to my wife Merideth whose constant wisdom, loyalty and support have done so much to facilitate the development of my own career.

Introduction

This book is about creating and maintaining a positive and realistic perspective on an academic career, about getting your career under control and keeping it there, and about building productive and fulfilling relationships with colleagues. It is intended for a variety of readers: newly appointed faculty members, graduate students and teaching assistants who are considering an academic career, and seasoned players who are looking for re-invigoration or a different point of view. Deans and heads of departments may also find this book useful as a source of ideas, especially for advising colleagues about the character of academic life and options for career development.

When academics take up positions at universities or colleges, they are commonly given a short orientation program. This typically involves introductions to the key people in the department and the university; an outline of institutional policies, procedures, and organisational structures; a tour of the campus; and some idea of where to go for help. Along with other appointees, beginning academics may also attend a familiarisation workshop and be given an induction handbook for reference.

Managing Your Academic Career covers those important things that are not in the induction handbook, and which a faculty member is supposed to just pick up along the way. It should enable a recent appointee to navigate through the system and maintain a clear vision of what academic life is supposed to be about.

Although institutions set many of the parameters for carrying out academic work, for a large part of their daily activities no one supervises faculty members closely. They have a significant degree of personal autonomy in relation to how they develop priorities. This particular feature of academic life, which can be both liberating and disquieting at the same time, is shared with many other professionals and self-employed persons. Academic work, however, takes place in a unique environment in a special kind of enterprise. The nature of this work lies essentially in disseminating, renewing, preserving and extending knowledge. For this to occur effectively, academics need to have a sense of direction and enough resources, elbow room, collegial support and time to do the job properly. When they get their priorities right, job satisfaction rises, and the system provides rewards in the form of promotion, tenure or other benefits. When they get them wrong, disillusionment, discouragement and boredom often follow.

To play the academic game effectively requires an understanding of the context and the rules. Fortuitous circumstances do play a part, of course, but so do organisation, self-discipline and good timing. Persuasion, skill, wisdom and tact are often indispensable ingredients. Most academics work hard and love what they do: the teaching, the interaction with colleagues and the sense of contributing to the generation of knowledge. They are often captivated by their chosen discipline and put in long hours. This, however, is not always enough. Being sensitive to basic academic values and working within institutional constraints are two of the keys to success—not in the sense of having status or of exercising power over others, but of enjoying academic work and having one's efforts and achievements recognised and rewarded.

Except in a few places, most of the book is written in the form of letters or memoranda to hypothetical early-career faculty members. Almost all these letters have their roots in real memoranda, personal conversations with colleagues, and questions raised at professional development seminars. They reflect the way I see things, and therefore my own values, priorities and prejudices. Because what makes for a successful career is open to interpretation, alternative perspectives and ways of doing things need to be evaluated. No single model or pattern will work for all circumstances. Readers will have to make their own decisions in the light of their career development to date, the character of the institution in which they work, and where they hope to be in the future. They will also need to allow for their personal circumstances, such as the ability to take up opportunities whenever and wherever they arise, family commitments, the need for security, and their tolerance of risk.

In recent years, higher education systems in many countries have been characterised by turbulence and uncertainty. Burgeoning student numbers, severe funding restrictions and a philosophy of economic rationalism have led to marked changes in institutional expectations, academic conditions and patterns of employment. These have made it harder to plan for an academic career, simply because there is no formula that is certain to work under all conditions. Despite that, it still makes good sense to develop a personal career perspective, to position oneself strategically within one's chosen field, and to re-position periodically as circumstances change.

The advice given here is general rather than specific. What some readers regard as common knowledge or just plain commonsense may be new to others, depending on their degree of prior acculturation into the traditions of their field or institution. Typical career paths differ from discipline to discipline.

In some fields, undergraduate students often progress directly from undergraduate to graduate studies, complete their doctoral or advanced degree programs, work in research teams, and then move into academic posts. Except for the staging that comes with completion of each qualification or employment contract, the process is an almost continuous affair. In other disciplines, especially professional areas, new graduates may first move into work outside the university system. After several years of professional practice, they may decide to further their studies through courses taken part-time. Eventually, working in a college or university may appeal to them as a career shift. Whether the letters in this book apply directly to you or not, it is nevertheless important to understand the situations and challenges faced by colleagues in other departments.

Each letter is able to be read independently of the others. This is to allow for convenient browsing. The short title for each letter does not necessarily signal everything covered in that letter. In addition, some themes are touched upon in several letters. The index is the best guide to where the various issues are dealt with. The books listed in the bibliography contain specialised information on personal organisation, writing applications and turning the academic appraisal process into a positive experience.

If you are poised at the beginning of an academic career, this collection will encourage you to understand the context in which you are working, to think about career directions, to exercise initiative and power, and to gain more satisfaction from academic life. Don't be overwhelmed by all there is to know; simply dip into the book whenever the need arises. I hope you find it interesting and useful.

D. Royce Sadler
Griffith University, Brisbane

Part one

ACADEMIC LIFE

Defining your academic focus

Dear Chris,

Congratulations on landing your new job! You asked for some frank advice on getting yourself started along the academic road. This is how I see things.

First of all, you need to become quite focused, channelling your reading, thinking, your research and your writing so that you are able to go deep into your field. If you want the experience and the excitement of being with the front-runners, you cannot afford to spread yourself too thinly. This is imperative for all academics: those who have just completed their PhDs after studying more or less continuously since their undergraduate years, those who have been working in a professional field before joining the academic ranks, and those with other backgrounds entirely.

Think carefully about your interests and academic commitments, including your teaching assignments and the terms of your appointment. Focus on what seems to be the essence of these, and work towards putting a short descriptive label on your main area of interest. This is what I refer to as an 'academic patch'. Matters outside the patch may well be interesting, but you should not allow them to assume too much importance. The patch itself is the thing.

The patch needs to have enough scope and variety to keep you fascinated and ensure your ability to cross-fertilise from one sub-area to another, but not be so extensive that you risk losing the plot or becoming seriously sidetracked. If you set the parameters of your interest too broadly, your patch may include too much and be unwieldy. If the parameters you set are too narrow, it may be too small for you to work in satisfactorily. You could then exhaust that field fairly quickly—or at least temporarily run out of challenging problems, and perhaps lose interest and enthusiasm. In general, avoid areas that are so esoteric that they could limit your future employment opportunities.

In your case, you have come into academic life after working in your profession. Defining a focus in this way may at first appear to draw you too far away from the interests of your former colleagues and the group of practitioners who may eventually become your graduate students. On the other hand, you are clearly aware of the problems that your profession is facing. The roots of those problems could well be tied up with inadequate conceptualisations of what the fundamental concerns really are. Often, practitioners struggle to put certain ideas into practice, unaware that the ideas themselves are flawed or incoherent.

Your combination of professional experience and theoretical knowledge gives you a valuable perspective. Many practitioners have a suspicion of theory and theorising, and there is some justification for that. They see it as mumbo jumbo, having no relevance to the real world and its problems. There is obviously a sense in which theorising, if it is too abstract and removed from the world of practice, is unable to contribute anything much to the field. However, there are other kinds of theorising that academics are ideally placed to pursue—mainly because of their training, but also because of the expectations in a university setting and the resources available to them. Faculty members often have at their fingertips the facilities—including a supportive environment and a reward system—that promote serious scholarship.

Some of this professional scholarship could, and should, be disseminated through academic journals. These provide a real test of its coherence, logical consistency, and power. On the other hand, if that knowledge remains purely at the academic level, it is unlikely to influence or be appreciated by the profession at large. You may find it useful, therefore, to run parallel streams of dissemination: one for an academic audience, the other for a professional audience. Both streams would need to have intellectual integrity, but would be shaped specifically for the differing needs of the two groups.

If you do decide to pursue one direction rather than many, here are a few more suggestions. The first is to burn bridges with the other areas that have interested you in the past, and be fairly ruthless about it. Otherwise they may function as an attractive diversion when things get difficult in your chosen domain. Where these other interests involve colleagues, you may have to explain to those colleagues what you are doing, and seek their understanding. This would reduce the possibility that your actions could be misinterpreted as being unfriendly or unsupportive. Your colleagues may be surprised initially, but I think most of them would, given time, come to respect your reasoning. I am always intrigued when I look through the research interests nominated by a group of academics. Some people have lists that go on forever. I suspect that many of those long lists signal a lack of focus and academic direction rather than a true breadth of expertise and vision.

Second, maintain this focus, as far as possible, in your teaching responsibilities. That way, you will build up a high level of expertise over a number of years. In the normal course of events, opportunities may arise for you to teach in generalist courses offered by your department, or to present specialist guest lectures in other programs. Balance these opportunities with a primary concentration on the area you were appointed to teach in. Your learning curve is likely to be quite steep for the first few years, despite the extent of your previous studies. As a broad generalisation, the more expert a person becomes in their chosen field, the more interested and enthusiastic they are. These qualities will have a significant impact on students. Of course, teaching for other courses can be rewarding, and preparing for a guest lecture is often a good opportunity to develop a bird's-eye view of key issues in your field. All I am saying is that you are not obliged to accept every invitation to teach outside your primary field.

Third, be strategic in your involvement with projects and external consultancies. Colleagues will no doubt be calling on you for specialised help with their projects. Opportunities of this type can provide excellent experience on the research front while you are developing your own profile. Project management, research techniques and report writing or publishing can all benefit from close interaction with highly skilled experts. Ultimately, however, you need to focus on your own research agenda. This could be compromised if you are always prepared to put your energy at the disposal of other established researchers. It would also raise their expectations about your future availability.

Involvement in external consultancies can be useful, however. They can help academics in the professional areas maintain contact with their field, and so feed on the source of many important social, scientific and professional issues. They shift your focus beyond the ivory tower. They also make high-level expertise available to the wider community, which is part of our more general social obligation as academics. On a more mundane note, they may provide funds for conference travel, general research infrastructure, and part-time employment for graduate students.

Obviously, the sponsors' external consultancies pay to have their own problems attended to first and foremost. Sometimes an academic is expected to provide a great deal of hackwork for the sponsor without a commensurate academic return. The sponsor should come to see that an academic who runs an agenda in tandem with that of the sponsor poses no threat, but helps set up a win-win situation. Personally, I am not drawn to being a well-paid research assistant for an outside agency unless I can see some potential for having my own thinking challenged and extended. This may be in terms of methodology, insights into policy and policy-making, or the establishment of more general (and generalisable) knowledge of which the sponsor's issue is a particular illustrative case. Mostly, sponsors have little difficulty with this.

Fourth, experiment with ways of attracting future graduate students to your area. You already have the primary ingredients: enthusiasm and an infectious way of seeing each problem as an occasion for progress. Some of your undergraduate students will be captivated by this. It is quite appropriate for you to suggest to a few of the most promising students, even halfway through their degrees, that undertaking graduate work should be added to their list of options to consider after graduation. Seeds sown early often bear fruit, even years later. Also, keep your eyes open while involved in your own consultancies and projects. A practitioner you interview, for example, may well be attracted to doing further study. Keep your entries in departmental and university directories informative and up to date so that people who search them (using the Internet, for example) can identify your research patch, and hence you.

Fifth, set yourself some goals to be achieved in relation to your patch. This may be in terms of articles to be published within a fixed time frame, reconstruction of the courses you teach, or something equally concrete. Specific goals, even if they are modest, help focus the mind. When you begin to achieve them, increased motivation will follow quickly.

Finally, avoid thinking of your academic patch, as you eventually define it, as a lifelong commitment. No one would expect you to pursue it relentlessly and single-mindedly for the rest of your life unless you keep making substantial progress and it suits your interests. As with doctoral studies, you have to be interested in it, to some extent passionately so, to make much headway.

Consider committing yourself to a definite plan of action for, say, a three-year or five-year term and see how far you get. Even in that relatively short period, you should be able to contribute something of significance to the field, and also to generate a love of serious scholarship that comes only by developing a commanding knowledge of the area, and being near the cutting edge yourself. Down the track a bit, it is always open to you to reassess and change direction, but first give yourself a realistic span of time to really get going.

2

Managing your time

Dear Geoff,

You asked for my suggestions on how to manage time. Most academics want to work efficiently and productively. As you might expect, the successful ones tend to be fairly hard-nosed about how they balance all the competing demands that are made upon them.

The 'time' issue should not, however, be seen in isolation. I sometimes run a half-hour workshop for colleagues on career priorities, and use a 'Ten Tips' handout (reproduced on pages 14–16) to focus the discussion. I begin with this for two reasons. The obvious one is that Tip 7 specifically deals with time management. But time management must be seen against the background of other issues and priorities, so that you can work out what you most want to *make time for*. If you look through the other nine tips, I think you'll see my point. You can't manage time effectively if you have only a hazy idea about your context, and about what you want to achieve.

A lot of faculty members feel constantly exasperated about

how time evaporates right before their eyes. However, university life is characterised by a great deal of personal freedom in how we as academics organise our time, and how much (and how) we interact with other people. Assuming we don't have a personal assistant, we also have to know a lot that is non-academic, because we act as our own office administrator, keyboarder, diary manager, letter writer, phone answerer, mail opener, document filer, and organiser of meetings and appointments. How can we find ways to preserve time for ourselves to think, to read, to research and to write?

As a first step, I suggest that you carry out a time audit over a typical week. You will probably be surprised at where your time goes. The audit will show you, in a concrete way, your *actual* present priorities. This is true simply by definition, even if you would want to argue that your current time allocations are dictated almost entirely by influences outside your control. If you really claim to have different priorities, you have to make the actual usage of time correspond with your ideal.

For example, friends who knock on the door and want to discuss an urgent problem for 'just one minute' can, over a period of time, deplete both your energy and the opportunity to engage in your own personal research and writing. You have to develop strategies that allow you to say 'no', or to be unavailable on call, without appearing unfriendly or reclusive. Part of good time management is working out schemes that protect time for important activities.

The university clearly expects you to prepare for teaching activities, to attend all scheduled lectures, tutorials and laboratory sessions, and to be available for several hours each week for consultation by students. All the formal commitments, such as classes and laboratory sessions, are listed in your weekly timetable. At those times, obviously, you are not available for casual discussions, to respond to e-mail, or to answer the phone. What does the rest of your weekly schedule look like on paper? Is it blank? Does it just fill up by itself? Or do you simply work from a 'To Do' list? I found I needed a systematic way to orchestrate my work week intelligently.

Most universities are keenly interested in the research output of their faculty members. This entirely legitimates your scheduling into your week specific times for research, whether you do it in your office, at home, in the laboratory, in the field, or in the library. If you are teaching in a lecture theatre, you cannot be interrupted by other colleagues in person or through technology. The structure of the system protects you and your students. Your research time should be just as highly protected, but you have to develop your own protection system. Make it impossible to be interrupted. I have found several effective strategies.

In my diary, I nominate specific times for research, setting them for a few days ahead. I decide what I will be working on and write in the actual project title, not something generic like 'research'. In the past, I found it hard to say 'no' to a colleague or student if I was staring at blank space in my diary, so now I get in first. If someone wants to make an appointment within a time I have already allocated, I explain: 'Sorry, I can't make it on Tuesday until noon. I will be tied up all morning with the Standards Policy Project.' No ifs and buts. We then examine our diaries until we find a mutually convenient time. Mostly that works fine. If all else fails, I am prepared to juggle things a bit but still look to find a way of moving intact blocks of time around.

I similarly allocate specific time for teaching preparation. I know roughly how much time I need each week, but I try to organise myself away from a strictly hand-to-mouth approach. A thorough knowledge of what I am teaching does a lot not only for my own interest in the topic but also for my self-confidence. Furthermore, there is clear research evidence that students learn more and react positively to a teacher who has a strong command over the subject matter and is enthusiastic about it. My self-confidence (and probably my performance as a teacher) tends to decay, however, if I do the specific preparation too far in advance of classes or, worse still, rely on last year's preparation. So for me timing is important.

I work best at thinking and writing in the mornings or late at night. Afternoons are not my strong time. So I try to schedule library visits and meetings with groups or individuals for after lunch. Also, conditions within my office vary some-what with time of day: sun movement, light and shadow, reflection from the computer screen or whiteboard. I set my research or thinking times for when personal and ambient conditions are best. I similarly schedule time for meeting preparation and working through the in-tray.

Technology is quickly moving to make us almost con-stantly accessible, so I have had to take steps to hold the line on my time allocation. For example, when I want no inter-ruptions at all, I set my phone on voice-mail and then unplug it from the wall. That way I do not even hear the phone ring, but the voice-mail system operated by the central university switchboard still works. Occasionally, I record a message that tells callers I am unavailable in my office at present but will be available during a certain period later in the day. Callers can still leave a message if they wish, but many don't. When they do call me back, they can be sure of being able to make contact.

My office computer is networked. Ordinarily, e-mail mes-sages are automatically flagged with a screen message as they arrive, and a little tune plays. When I am concentrating on my research or writing, I either disable the e-mail arrival message or use my local software without logging into the network at all. I cannot then be distracted by incoming e-mail arrival, or tempted to stop work to see what is in the message. The e-mail has to wait. Faxes I treat as ordinary mail, not necessarily as immediate priorities. In many cases, faxes are not urgent but are used for convenience instead of ordinary mail. I also watch the time I spend on the Internet, trying not to follow all the interesting links.

My time audit showed I wasted a lot of time looking for things, leafing through the same familiar piles of stuff, sometimes several times on the one day. To avoid this, I found out from a competent secretary how to create a Bring Forward filing system. Material for all future meetings is now filed when I receive it according to the date of the meeting. Filing practice is a topic in its own right. Talk with some of your researcher colleagues to find out how they file and index their collections of journal articles, their books and periodicals, and their other materials. Before launching into a computer database for indexing your material, ask around to see whether it is worth doing by computer at all. I tried it once, but found myself spending so much time keeping the database up to date that I abandoned it. I now file my material in several broad categories by author. I can nearly always find what I am looking for within one minute.

The audit also showed that I spent too much time socialising over coffee, and checking my mailbox morning and afternoon each day, immediately after deliveries. Coffee breaks with colleagues are vital for most of us to keep up personal friendships and to find out what's going on in the department. Being present at every break, however, is unnecessary. So scheduling attendance at departmental coffee breaks is a sensible option. The significance of the 'frequency equation' referred to in Tip 7 is just this: regular interaction with colleagues four times each week can be as productive as eight. Advertisers know that an advertisement in a weekly magazine every alternate week is just as effective for sales as a weekly ad, but costs only half as much overall.

Academic work is characterised by special forms of open-endedness. Although we are employees, there is no limit to how much time we *could* put into preparation for teaching, and no limit to how much we *could* put into research and writing. Conscientious academics often find their work expanding to demand all evenings, the weekends and even vacations. We ourselves have a major responsibility for setting limits and working within them, and we ourselves are responsible for ensuring that the energy we do have is put into high priority areas.

Whole books have been written on time management, usually from a business perspective. Some of this, particularly the principles if not all the detail, can be translated into the academic environment. I'll leave the rest to your own ingenuity.

TEN TIPS FOR ESTABLISHING PRIORITIES

1. *Understand your context*
   What is your background? Where do you want to be in five years' time? Who are likely to be your research and publishing colleagues? Are they motivated?
2. *Determine how strongly you WANT to be a scholar-researcher-teacher*
   If the drive is not there, maybe you should look for a different opportunity for your skills and qualifications.
3. *Seize control of your environment*
   Refuse to see yourself as a victim, discriminated against because of your inexperience or background or in any other way subject to vague external forces. Once you have seized control, retain it.
4. *Know yourself*
   Are you essentially a team player or a loner? What are your skills and strengths in managing things, in personality, in intellectual style, in world view, in working with others? What are your foibles and weaknesses? What things give you confidence and a sense of satisfaction?

What things intrigue you? What are the things or people that waste time, divert your attention, decrease your motivation and sense of purpose, or reduce your self-confidence? Is perfectionism reducing your effectiveness?

5. *Build systems*

   Build systems to reinforce your strengths and overcome your deficiencies. It does not matter how weird or corny the systems may appear to others. You do not owe them an explanation. Create systems to track your progress as well as systems to keep you on target and motivated.

6. *Set specific achievement targets*

   Set targets that involve multiple outcomes. Be prepared to adapt and weave about. Develop alternative goals so that if blockage occurs in one direction you can make progress in another. Keep your academic focus appropriately narrow, and aim high in terms of scholarship and rigour. Generate a program of research and writing, not a series of single shots that do not combine to advance your scholarship and sense of progression.

7. *Manage your time*

   Build research and writing time into your daily and weekly planning, and regard them as appointments that are as fixed as your classes are. Plan as systematically for research and publication as you do for your classes, teaching preparation or committee meetings. Also plan your socialising: morning and afternoon teas, lunch times, collecting the mail. Understand the frequency equation. Work from an appointments diary or day-sheet, not a teaching timetable.

8. *Recognise the cycles in academic life*

   At any one time, only a couple of activities might be at the forefront. Schedule appropriate activities according to time of day, period of semester, time of year and outside (including family) responsibilities. Balance periods for critical thought with time for mechanical activities.

9. *Support your colleagues in their endeavours*
   Academic life can be pretty lonely and stressful. Be generous in encouragement, but give praise only when it is warranted.

10. *Enjoy your successes*
    Use your successes to maintain confidence and momentum. Do not fret about waiting; organise other things to do. Be patient with yourself.

3

Finding a mentor

Dear Llarno,

Many academics sense the need for some sort of role model or mentor, especially after they have settled into their new positions. Once they are over the initial hurdles relating to their formal responsibilities, the time comes when they start to reflect on where they are heading, and how they can best manage the process. There is no doubt that the opportunity to work with other, more senior, academic colleagues can be both satisfying and highly effective.

In some universities, mentoring relationships are formalised through the department chair as a kind of 'senior buddy' arrangement. Where these programs exist, the compatibility of the two people is of paramount importance. The idea of having just one mentor means that the more experienced person has to have a special array of attributes. The match is important, and finding the right person can sometimes be difficult. Compatibility applies not only to personality, but also to perspectives on academic work and values generally.

You might find that you could bring up the idea with your department chair, and play a part in helping other academics develop mentoring relationships. Formal schemes do carry some risks: some work well, others don't. They may have even been tried before you arrived and been abandoned, or just fizzled out of their own accord. If your department does go ahead in developing mentoring as a project, make sure it does its homework beforehand. A substantial amount of literature on academic mentoring exists, with lots of pointers on things to avoid and procedures to maximise its effectiveness.

I gather from what you have said that no arrangements are in place at present. Here are six points to think about:

1. Don't be deterred at all. You might actually be better served in the absence of a formal program, because you can stay in the driver's seat.
2. You don't need a person's permission to look on them as a role model. Just do it.
3. Figure out where you need help or a model. Designing new curriculum? Developing expertise in teaching? Expanding or updating research skills? Managing a research team? Applying for research grants? Motivation for a higher degree? Administrative skills? Career development? Academic rejuvenation? Balancing academic and personal priorities?
4. Don't limit yourself to seeking out a single mentor. Learn from several colleagues by putting together your own composite mentor. You can do it in a low-key, informal way with faculty members whose values you respect. Talk to them. Find out what you can about their career history, their aspirations, their academic orientation and outlook, and what principles determine their academic priorities. Although the most likely prospect is someone in your own field or department, don't overlook the possibility of someone elsewhere in the university. You might meet

someone at the university club at lunch times. You could even use someone outside the university altogether.

5. Have a few specific ideas on how you might be best helped. For example, a mentor might be prepared to let you peruse actual reviewers' reports on some manuscripts for journal articles, together with the ensuing correspondence with the editor that led to publication in their final form. Other possibilities include student evaluations of teaching, successful and unsuccessful grant applications, and the mentor's curriculum vitae.

6. Take your cues from high achievers, people who know the ropes through experience. Make sure their approach is one that is compatible with your own values, including attitudes to advancement. There are many ways of getting to the top, but here are two extremes. The first is through sheer quality of work: excellence in teaching, seminal presentations at conferences, high-achieving graduate students, and publications that are highly original, break new ground, and are widely cited. The other is to work what I call the 'influence field' for all it is worth: attend every conference going (costly!), talk up what you are doing, know everybody on a first-name basis, drop important names everywhere, and cultivate a personal coterie of loyal colleagues whose support and recommendations you can rely on. Although I recognise that personal contact with significant scholars necessarily plays an important role in academic advancement, my personal leaning is towards the former.

The above suggestions roughly parallel my own experience. As a young academic, I did not, at least consciously, search for a mentor. In fact, I had hardly heard the word then. But I did recognise an affinity with two other academics in particular, both of whom were considerably more advanced in their careers than I was. This is what impressed me about them. They both had high academic ability and integrity; were productive as researchers; had great respect for their students; were concerned about good teaching; and promoted the causes of their graduate students, without exploiting them. Further, they resisted intellectual bandwagons, which meant that they were courageous and not afraid to take distinctive positions on fundamental issues, and then defend them. They also seemed to be able to manage their personal and professional lives, and achieve a balance between academic and non-academic activities. In other words, they weren't academic hermits. Both were very generous and encouraging in helping me sort through some muddled ideas I had when I first began publishing in academic journals. That type of generosity was itself something I was greatly impressed with and have since tried to emulate. Neither of these two role models was from my own university.

What I have outlined above are two extremes: the formal, departmentally based mentor arrangement and the informal do-it-yourself scheme. There is also a path in the middle. It involves having the department head's office operate as a confidential clearing house. Experienced academics who are willing to act as mentors, and other academics who are looking for a mentor, send independent signals to the head's office. The inexperienced faculty members also indicate their area of greatest need. The department head then facilitates connections between the potential mentors and mentorees in a way that leaves no one embarrassed. This approach is worth serious consideration, because some relatively junior members may feel sensitive or uneasy about approaching a possible mentor directly. Conversely, experienced faculty members may be prepared to act as a mentor but aren't sure how to make this availability known.

This gives you three possibilities to think about. You will need to work out something that suits your own circumstances.

4

Establishing an academic network

Dear Thaissen,

It was great to hear that you will be presenting your first paper at an international conference later this year. The conference theme sounds fascinating. You can be pretty sure that the three keynote speakers will address themselves more or less to the theme, but don't have too high expectations about the rest of the papers!

What usually happens at 'open' conferences, where anyone who chooses can register and attend, is that only half the presenters take the theme seriously. Some of the others wangle a few key words from the theme into their text. The rest simply ignore the theme and deliver a paper about what they are interested in and have been researching. Ordinarily, you will have the conference program ahead of time, so you can choose among the parallel sessions to suit your own needs. If some of the abstracts printed in the program seem only tenuously related to the paper that is actually delivered, that is par for the course.

Invitational conferences are different; so are those focused on a restricted research area. Both of these, in any case, usually have relatively small numbers of delegates attending.

It is always exciting to meet some of the people whose work you have found important in your own research. This is a good time for you to begin establishing connections with other scholars in your field. After all, you are not just interested in what they have done, you have something to offer as well. You said you already know of several key researchers who will be going to the conference. Naturally, you want to meet them, and hear what they are working on.

It is a good idea, well before the conference, to make preliminary contact with a few of them. That way you can look out for one another. If you leave everything until you get there, you might find that the conference is all but over before you find an opportunity to make contact. The opening informal drinks session is usually useful for connecting, so do a bit of targeting. I hope the name tags are legible at a good distance. If they're not, ask around. At one conference I went to, the name tags supplied were in minuscule printing, so I rewrote mine to be legible from half a mile away. Some stranger came up and asked me if I had an identity problem. Couldn't read who it was!

Actually, serious academic correspondence between researchers in many disciplines is relatively infrequent. They all seem to know about one another's work. They make use of it when they need to, and also cite it. But they just don't keep up much personal contact. I am surprised at this, although e-mail has changed the situation a lot in recent years. It would be interesting to know how much specifically scholarly mail the leaders in your field receive. Often it is very little. If the opportunity arises, ask a couple of them at the conference. My experience has been that most scholars are very willing to discuss their own work with other researchers, provided the inquirers are serious and not simply curious. When contact is made, it is certainly very welcome.

On several occasions, I have run a discussion group with colleagues here at this university on how to establish what I call, for want of a better name, a personal academic network. I put together a few tips on how to go about it, which you can read below. I don't say that this is a foolproof approach, but it might give you some ideas on how to start. I think you will find it self-explanatory.

All the best for getting your conference paper together.

TEN TIPS FOR ESTABLISHING A PERSONAL ACADEMIC NETWORK

1. *Identify a small number of potential scholarly colleagues.* They will most likely be the researchers whose work you make most use of. Be bold. Don't be overawed. Approach great names if (and only if) they are central figures in your research field, but assume they are already very busy. By the same token, don't overlook beginning researchers in your area, people with a fresh approach or challenging ideas.

2. *Assume that your potential colleagues are favourably disposed towards academic interaction.* Most will be, particularly if your fields of activity are broadly coincident. Many welcome debate and discussion, and are open to diverse points of view. Relatively little genuine interaction goes on outside formal exchanges in journals. Yet most researchers like to talk about their work.

3. *Work at building up enduring professional relationships.* Be prepared to persevere without being pushy or painful. Know when to back off.

4. *Do your homework.* Check that your potential colleagues are still alive, and find their current title and institutional

affiliation. Get the details exact. Use the various directories to national and international universities in the library, or search the Internet. Know thoroughly what they have written. Don't ask them for a list of their publications; you can find that out through a CD-ROM search in your library. And definitely don't ask for copies of 'all their other publications' either!

5. *Consider using ordinary mail in the first instance.* Don't underestimate what can be achieved this way. It is very effective, and reaches almost everywhere. But by all means capitalise on meeting people at conferences if you are able to attend any.

6. *Connect yourself.* Explain the significance of their research to you and your work. Indicate what you are working on. Express interest and appreciation, but stop short of flattery. Feel at liberty to challenge a result or perspective, but do it sensitively and constructively. Ask specific questions about applications, extensions, extrapolations and clarifications.

7. *Contribute to the interactions.* Take an active role in cross-linking ideas, references and contacts. Contribute a relevant journal article if you have one. But don't send great volumes of your own work, especially reports and conference papers. You can safely assume they won't read the material.

8. *Prepare the ground for the first personal contact.* Don't wait for a conference or flying visit. Set each contact up, but also follow through after a conference or visit.

9. *Plan for contact several times a year.* Keep communications brief, to the point and at an academic rather than personal level until a social relationship exists. Avoid the fax; things are seldom that urgent. E-mail provides an informal and effective way to keep in contact, especially after some sort of rapport is established.

10. *Expect the full range of personality characteristics.* Your new contact may be arrogant, friendly, crabby, egotistical, shy, retiring, narrow-minded, charismatic, belligerent, unassuming, brilliant, broad-minded or boring.

5

Performing on a selection committee

Dear Phil,

As the elected representative of junior academics on a selection committee to appoint a full professor, you certainly do have a voice that must be heard. Don't let your lack of experience make you feel you have nothing to contribute. Some of the committee members will be there mainly because of their seniority in the university hierarchy, but they do not necessarily have intimate knowledge of the workings of your department. Your perspective is important because you know about the real needs of administrative and academic colleagues, and of students.

Being a full member of a senior committee will also provide you with valuable experience as to how they work. You will have the same access to the applications and to the confidential referee's reports as other committee members, and your vote will count equally.

Your own thinking will be based on your reading of their applications, the reports, and a perusal of the key publications nominated by each candidate. The essential consideration is how the short-listed candidates measure up to the selection criteria, and that is an area where you can contribute. Some of the committee members may know some of the applicants personally, but that should not be allowed to get in the way of a sound decision. Despite your lack of first-hand knowledge about any of the candidates, it is perfectly in order for you to draw attention to the primary selection criteria as the deliberations proceed. This is not just you speaking; the selection criteria were set by others prior to advertisement.

You said that your department currently has only twelve faculty members, and is in the process of rebuilding its teaching and research profile after the retirement of several leading lights during the past two years. The advertisement and the information packets sent to potential applicants emphasised that scholarly leadership is important in this appointment. This obviously includes providing leadership in teaching. The non-academic attributes of the candidates, including their people skills and their personalities, are qualities which will influence their effectiveness in the department and, ultimately, the reputation of the department.

WITH RESPECT TO TEACHING

- Look for evidence of high-quality teaching in courses at different levels. Many applicants give this aspect only cursory attention, even when it is stated explicitly in the selection criteria.
- Look for evidence of substantial commitment to high-quality teaching, and their record of supporting good teaching in colleagues. Absence of firm data on this, or even its omission from the application, may imply that teaching is a low priority for them.
- Look for an awareness of what each candidate sees as the

most significant challenges facing university teaching at present.

WITH RESPECT TO RESEARCH

- Look for breadth as well as depth. This does not necessarily mean that the best candidate will have a number of distinct directions in their research, but their records should show an awareness of other fields, a proven ability to bring quite different perspectives to bear on fundamental questions, and significant contributions in both the substantive domain (empirical research and theory development) and in the methodology domain (research techniques and evaluation of methods).
- Look for quality as well as quantity. A number of the publications should be outstanding in terms of their impact on the field and be part of an integrated research program. A good proportion should be published in journals of high international repute, and at least some should be widely cited.
- Because yours is a professional field, look for connections with professional practitioners, with some of the research being influenced by fieldwork and by a concern to retain a connection with what might be called applicable research.

WITH RESPECT TO PERSONAL QUALITIES

- Look for a person who is not only expert in their discipline but also capable of acting as a spokesperson for their discipline and their profession generally. This is important in the appointment of a full professor, especially when there are to be just two in the department.
- Look for a person whose application indicates high levels

of international collegiality that could be built on to benefit the department.

- Look for the ability to mentor and enthuse less senior faculty members, such as yourself. This is just as relevant as orchestrating a personal or team research agenda.

You may find that a lot of the discussion tends to swirl around research performance, because in some senses this is easier to evaluate than, say, teaching performance. A further consideration is that the university as an institution, which will no doubt be represented by a number of senior faculty members from other disciplines, may lean towards appointing a person who will raise the research profile and grant-getting capacity of the university. If this occurs, it is appropriate for you to bring the committee's attention back to the explicitly stated selection criteria, including demonstrated teaching performance.

Finally, the field of applicants may not include anybody who is outstanding on all major selection criteria. That would not be surprising, and may involve a discussion of which candidate represents the best compromise. With your input about those areas in which the department needs leadership most, you can help the committee appoint the person whose performance profile across all fronts appears to offer the greatest long-term benefit for your department.

6

Designing a sabbatical

Dear Kerry,

Where it is available, a period of sabbatical leave is a superb provision. It goes by all sorts of different names, and regulations vary widely, but almost always it is regarded as a privilege rather than as a right. For many academics, their first period of sustained release from teaching, committees and other academic duties enables them to launch their own independent scholarship in a significant way.

You asked me a lot of questions about setting up contacts with colleagues in other universities, and negotiating about working conditions in other academic environments and cultures. I will put off making suggestions on these until I have made a few preliminary comments. Sorting out practical arrangements is something that should follow rather than lead your basic design for the sabbatical, and it's the design that I want to start with.

First, I suggest you set yourself some realistic goals about what you intend to achieve, then plan the arrangements so that there is a high probability of bringing these to fruition. Without definite objectives and targets, you might find—as many have in the past—that time just slips away. You could find yourself busy all the time, enjoying the academic energy and direction of colleagues, and undoubtedly broadening and deepening your knowledge and skills in the process. At the end of the day, however, you might have little that is concrete to show for it, particularly in relation to scholarship, research and writing. A sabbatical is a golden opportunity to accomplish things that otherwise either would not be achieved at all or would take years.

These targets may be in terms of resources to be researched, produced or written for a new course you will be teaching, a book manuscript to be developed and partly written, or several journal articles to be finalised or substantially drafted. The primary purpose of doing this detailed thinking about what you can realistically achieve is so that you have a clear academic agenda for your sabbatical. It also means that, if your application is approved, you can do specific preparatory work and so get yourself up to speed as much as possible before the sabbatical begins officially. This would allow you to make best use of the opportunity. Preparing might involve doing preliminary reading, collecting resources, preparing materials or sorting out ideas.

I am sure you have heard innumerable times about the advantages of having a broad goal with a set of related specific objectives, of writing them down, and of being systematic in working towards them, so I won't labour the point. It is, however, a curious irony that so many people know this in theory but never put it into practice.

It is important to be realistic. Some applicants for special studies leave have grand plans about what they expect to achieve but have no previous record of success in those areas. It is as though they believe their total lack of performance in the past has been due to a complete lack of opportunity.

Sabbatical leave is somehow supposed to be able to work a miracle for them.

Having a clear and achievable academic agenda is important for another reason as well: it will make for a strong application. Some of the applications I have considered as a committee member have an almost exclusive focus on where the person wishes to go and the colleagues they hope to spend time with, accompanied by some glowing account of how all this will more or less turn the academic world upside down. What the committee is likely to look for is much more down to earth: what evidence is there that the proposed allocation of university funds in salary and allowances—a not inconsiderable sum in most cases—is likely to result in commensurate academic benefit to the individual, the work of the department and the university?

In my experience, committees are more likely to evaluate an application for a sabbatical program in terms of its potential as an investment in the future rather than how ambitious it is or whether the person deserves a reward for previous work. For this reason, and other things being equal, demonstrated productivity arising from a particular sabbatical increases the probability that a future application would also be successful.

With those comments as background, I will now turn to your specific issues. The overall consideration should be that you design your itinerary and activities so that you are best placed to achieve your objectives. In some cases, this could involve little or no travel at all.

I appreciate your interest in wanting to make contact with ten of the leading scholars in your field worldwide. I take it you mean contact in person, which implies you must have resources for fairly extensive travel. You will be the envy of most of the colleagues you visit! The only reservation I have is that 'making contact' with many scholars is not as beneficial as establishing a solid professional relationship with a limited number of scholars on an enduring basis.

I once had a colleague who planned his study leave more or less along the lines you suggest. It was a real whistle-stop tour, and he was fortunate enough to get positive responses back from most of the researchers he wrote to. However, things didn't work out quite the way he had hoped.

When he got to Chicago, for example, he found that the eminent researcher he had planned to meet with was actually out of the country at the time, but had arranged for a doctoral candidate to host him for the two days he was at the university. The doctoral student was also a teaching assistant who was very busy, because it was near the end of semester. When my friend arrived in New York, the key person he was to visit was tied up chairing a high-level inquiry into academic salaries. Later on, my colleague was in London for three days, but the researcher he met up with there was only able to spare him half an hour or so, not really enough time to establish any relationship at all. Variations on these experiences were repeated at most places he went. He did manage to make a few reasonable contacts, but often not with the people he originally wanted to see. He came back quite disillusioned with the whole exercise, and considerably in debt.

The most successful sabbaticals seem to be where a person spends a substantial period of time in a congenial environment, getting to know the faculty members, the context, and the local culture of the university and its community. This can be a useful starting point for continuing academic contact.

I suggest you think in terms of two or three places to visit, and work from there. These places should involve researchers with whom you already have a fair bit in common. If you are granted another sabbatical some time in the future, you could make shorter visits to those same centres if the earlier academic exchanges have been fruitful, because the groundwork will have been done.

In writing to potential contacts, you would obviously want to test the academic environment. It would also be useful to ask some pretty mundane questions about such matters as the availability and cost of housing, and whether your children would have to pay fees to go to the local school. I was forced to reschedule some of my plans on one occasion when I discovered that the going rate for housing was about six times what I would get for my own house if I leased it out for the period I would be away. I would have gone broke in the process!

Have modest expectations about space and equipment needs. Don't ask the people at the other end to find housing or a vehicle or to make other domestic arrangements for you, unless they offer short-term solutions to assist you until you get settled. An inquiry about house sitting for absent faculty members might, however, prove productive.

It always takes a little time to work into the culture of a centre or department, even if the language of communication is English. Some prestigious centres and departments put up with a constant stream of academic visitors, simply because of their international reputations. Some of these visitors have what can only be described as vague reasons for calling; they just want to 'see what the centre is doing'. In some cases, the stream of visitors is so large that trying to do justice to them all would virtually disable the centre, which has to fully maintain its own normal activity, including its teaching commitments and meeting crucial project deadlines. There is a sense in which such visitors may feel that they are *processed*, rather than treated as visiting academics, but I am sure you can see how this could pose a real problem for a centre.

If you were to spend, say, two or more months in the one place, a lot of your academic exchange would probably take place through being involved in some of the research projects under way. This could involve acting as a sounding board for various project teams, contributing to field visits and data collection, and reading or editing parts of project reports or manuscripts for articles. Academic interaction also comes about through participating in some of the courses the centre teaches. You may be able to provide several advanced seminars for faculty members and graduate students, in which case you would need to take relevant materials with you. A lot of academic exchange, however, takes place informally through simply being there at coffee breaks and mealtimes.

If you have your own academic agenda to pursue, as I suggested above, it will give you something concrete to work on while being gradually introduced to the centre's activities. It also relieves the centre's members from feeling a sense of responsibility to keep you occupied.

To change tack a bit, I was warned by a sincere and well-meaning colleague when planning my first sabbatical that leading international researchers would most likely not be interested in an approach from an obscure person like myself, without a doctorate, and lowly ranked in the academic hierarchy. In fact, this was not a problem at all. On the contrary, I was impressed with how generously disposed towards me many high-profile academics were.

Being in tune with the potential hosts' styles of research is a definite advantage. That means being knowledgeable about their research itself as well as being on roughly the same wavelength in relation to methodology. Equally important, though, is having something different, interesting, and of academic significance to contribute yourself, and being able to relate to these colleagues sensibly and sensitively on a personal level.

Having said all that, let me encourage you to plan your study leave carefully, so that you get the maximum academic result from it. Make connections that will be productive for the future, and that set you up for a period of sustained activity until you have your next opportunity for concentrated research leave. Aim to make your first sabbatical something of a watershed in your academic development.

And, of course, enjoy yourself!

7

Writing research grant proposals

Dear Trudy,

You asked for a few tips on applying for research grants. All I can do in a letter is give you some sort of overview, and point in some general directions to get you started.

I am sure you are aware of the differences in research requirements across different disciplines. In a few fields, theoretical research can be carried out with quite modest facilities (say, writing materials, a small computer and access to a good library). But in many situations, external funding is absolutely necessary for the work to be carried out, for equipment, expertise, supplies, salaries and so on. A substantial grant over a three-year period, for example, allows a researcher to assemble a team consisting of faculty members, graduate students and research assistants to work on a major project.

Some grant application principles are general and apply more or less across all fields. Others apply to specific types of research. Two readily available sources of information are print materials (books and funding agency guidelines) and people (successful grant applicants in your department together with researchers who have experience as proposal assessors for funding agencies). In addition, you should not have any difficulty in locating one of the good, modern guides on writing proposals and bidding for research grants. These how-to books sometimes include actual samples of successful grant applications.

To explore what is available in print, start with your library and university research office. You should be able to find a copy of a comprehensive grants register (covering a wide range of fields, disciplines, industries and professions) without much trouble. The number of agencies is quite surprising. Some of them are quite small with not much visibility, but may be good sources nevertheless. Read carefully about the range of research areas they are prepared to sponsor. Don't assume it is as narrow as the name of the organisation might imply. For example, a fishing industry council may be prepared to sponsor research on a wide range of industry issues: health and safety of people at sea, international treaties and politics, psychological conditions for trawler crews and economic issues facing the industry, as well as more scientific problems to do with fish and fishing.

A good place to start when you are preparing to write a proposal is actually at the end point. Granting bodies often produce *Guidelines for Assessors*. Where these exist, they are usually quite explicit about the criteria and weightings that assessors are asked to apply to individual applications. I have just pulled out of my files a copy of the report forms sent to me by one of the granting agencies I review for. It asks me to give a numerical score on each of the following criteria:

- Priority for the granting organisation—the extent to which the aims of the proposed research are consistent with the interests of the funding body, including fulfilment of the stated conditions.

- Quality of the research proposal—originality of the design, the practical or theoretical significance of the expected results, the strength of the case made in the documentation.
- Calibre of the researcher or team—research record, qualifications, record of successful management of previous research projects.
- Probability of beneficial outcomes—the likelihood of a successful conclusion.

These might look distinct, but they do overlap somewhat. Basically, the funding body is asking each assessor for an opinion as to whether a strong enough case is made for the agency to fund the research. As you can see, an element of persuasion is involved. An argument that is well articulated and provides appropriate evidence and attention to detail has a better chance of success. Some of the most common problems with proposals are:

- The nature of the research is inappropriate to the granting agency's brief.
- What is being proposed is vague. The applicant writes lots of impressive words but the assessor cannot identify the nub of the problem or the hypotheses to be tested.
- There is a lack of appreciation of research in the field and of what has already been done, accompanied by sweeping statements about the critical need for further research.
- The budgeting is poorly conceived, with questionable costing (either ridiculously high or unrealistically low), insufficient justification and explanation for the budget items, and no allowance for buying in specialised expertise.
- The project-management ability of the principal researcher is uncertain.

Choosing an appropriate research problem is most important. For an academic, the proposed research should be relevant to the researcher's developing career theme, and not be just any project that will bring in funds. The scope of what is proposed should also reflect the researcher's level of experience. A request for two million dollars over three years for a new research program to be carried out by an inexperienced team will almost certainly be turned down. Previous well-managed pilot studies add credibility. Most successful researchers work their way up the financial scale.

Here are my remaining tips:

1. When writing the proposal, be knowledgeable about the field. Know what other relevant research has already been carried out. There are two reasons for this. First, duplicated research, unless with the specific purpose of replication, is wasteful. The second reason is political: the person whose work you overlook may be selected by the agency as the reviewer of your own proposal.

2. Outline what you have in mind clearly and succinctly. Indicate the theoretical underpinnings of your proposed study. State how your research will complement or extend the results from other research. Give details of the procedures you hope to use, the sequencing and the expected time line. Anticipate where things could wander outside the primary design and explain how you will adjust or cope in response.

3. Do your costing and budgeting carefully. Provide for actual costs (equipment, travel and accommodation, questionnaire mail out) plus adequate infrastructure (research assistance, office supplies, and consultants' fees where special expertise is required for specific purposes). Find out what the going rates are by getting actual salary ranges or commercial quotations where relevant. Your research office or personnel department can help with salaries and allowances. Take account of items that are explicitly exempted from additional research funding. These are

typically facilities that the funding agency assumes are part of the normal institutional infrastructure. Don't pad the budget, but allow for some contingencies.

4. Include a time budget for yourself; show how you will be able to allocate specific time to the project and continue to manage your other responsibilities.

5. Outline how you see the results of the research being disseminated or published.

6. Conform to the funding agency's protocols on ethical considerations for all experimentation involving human or animal subjects.

7. Conform meticulously with the funding agency's application procedures: lodgment deadline, maximum length of the document, upper budget limits, number of copies to be submitted and format of presentation (section headings, typeface, borders, line spacing and references). Some grant agencies run with an open timetable: researchers may apply at any time of the year. Others have definite grant rounds with advertised closing dates.

8. Finish writing the proposal early so you have time to run it past an experienced grant recipient for constructive feedback.

Finally, don't give up. Funding for research is often highly competitive, so a lot of applicants miss out. Don't take it hard. A general granting body often receives several times more applications than it can fund. Some of these will be successful by a large margin, others will miss by an equally large margin. In the middle are a whole lot of reasonable projects that could possibly be funded. The fate of many of these depends partly on the agency's choice of assessors and on the availability of these assessors soon after the closing date. If you receive assessors' reports after a decision not to fund, use them to overhaul the research project or to revise your proposal for resubmission at a later time or to another agency.

8

Changing academic fields

Dear Doyle,

I am interested to hear that you are thinking of making a shift to a different academic field. Some people do this to follow emerging research interests, some have it imposed on them, and others just seem to run out of steam in their original field and look for a new set of challenges.

The toughest decisions are faced by faculty members who are forced to either make a radical change or be declared redundant. This happens when a university decides to eliminate certain courses or departments in response to changing student demand, or simply to reduce faculty numbers to create space for new developments. You are fortunate not to be in that situation yourself, so you have more options open to you.

All fields probably have their examples of research areas that become defunct because of the lack of challenging worthwhile problems. I am always intrigued to look through journals of, say, fifty years ago and note how some of the things that we think are trivial today were once burning issues, and how other problems that appeared to be intractable then still seem intractable today. It's also humbling to see where others have been before.

Many professionals, academic and otherwise, find that their careers undergo several transformations during their lifetimes. Fifty years ago, major transitions like these were relatively rare, but they will constantly be increasingly common in the future. Survivors will need to be constantly attuned to change. For most of us, that is easier to talk about than to put into practice. Obviously, anyone who doggedly sticks with the same academic agenda will run a higher risk of redundancy than someone who can adapt. Being open to new opportunities and incremental change should help avoid the biggest jolts.

You say you have progressively lost enthusiasm for your area, and are looking to find greener pastures elsewhere—possibly even in another discipline. Don't despair too early. Many academics find that their careers go in cycles, with periods of high job satisfaction and productivity punctuated by low spots that may last as long as one or two years. Check that you are not simply in a low spot. What you clearly have in your favour is a high regard for academic life, an enviable reputation as a university teacher, and a history of conspicuous achievement in research. Those are substantial assets.

Shifting from one set of teaching responsibilities to teaching in another field may be a possibility, depending on circumstances. You should find this easier to negotiate within your own department than if you wanted to join another department altogether. Unless you already have standing teaching and research responsibilities in the other department, you would almost certainly have to wait until a vacancy occurs, then compete with applicants who are already highly qualified in that area.

Moving laterally to a new field within the same department

and the same broad discipline area is a different proposition. If you do decide to follow this line, the first step would be to signal this to your department head. Otherwise, if a sudden vacancy were to occur in the area you wanted to move into, an advertisement could be placed at very short notice for a replacement person. It would most likely be filled by an outside applicant. If you applied, you could naturally expect to face stiff competition and in the end be unsuccessful. Both you and the department could then have lost a good opportunity.

Any vacancy, properly handled, has the potential for creating an opportunity to review a range of interlinked academic responsibilities. Pieces of the jigsaw may be moved around to accommodate the aspirations of a number of faculty members at once. This is more likely to be successful if it is done openly, with no secret deals and no guaranteed commitments in advance. Eventually, the department will settle on the area where the newly identified vacancy exists. The department can still get its new blood, but at the same time help one or more of its existing academics to take up the new challenges they need.

A colleague of mine was once in the same sort of situation you are in, but the department head was unaware of my colleague's hopes of moving into a new field. A sudden resignation occurred, though in an area the colleague was not particularly interested in. Advertisements were placed immediately, and the vacancy filled. The new appointee brought optimism and vigour to the department, was an excellent teacher, attracted some good graduate students and in a short time had developed a strong research profile. On the surface, the department had done what was academically sound. The sad part was that no further vacancies in the department occurred for several years, and my colleague became progressively more disgruntled and unproductive. In hindsight, the situation could have been handled quite differently.

In another case, one that worked out well, the person who had to make the most radical shift in academic area was supported with a reduced teaching load for two years. This allowed the person to undertake graduate study in the new area, and then take up full teaching responsibilities. The result: one satisfied and invigorated academic. Whatever momentum the department had lost, it regained within a year or two. A new position was created in an emerging area, and filled by an outstanding scholar. This was redeployment at its best. Obviously, serendipity played a part, but the opportunity needed to be recognised and dealt with promptly and creatively. Bringing it to fruition required imagination, confidentiality at certain critical points, considerable diplomatic skills, and a high level of respect for colleagues.

In the absence of an event such as a resignation or retirement, a move to a new field may still be a possibility for you, especially if you do it in stages rather than attempt a sudden jump. Because of the tradition of research freedom in universities, there is probably nothing to stop you developing expertise, scholarship and a research program in a new area anyway. If ultimately you were to publish several high-quality articles, this would almost certainly be regarded as equivalent to having formal qualifications in the field. This could be achieved without threatening your, or anyone else's, current position in the department.

You would not want your colleagues to misinterpret your actions and motivations. The move would need to be planned and implemented tactfully with the full support of your department head, and carried out over a period of time. A disadvantage of doing it this way is that your teaching and research interests would gradually diverge unless a complementary scheme could be developed for refocusing your teaching at the same time.

Universities as a whole seem to be poorly prepared for helping academics migrate from one field to another in an enlightened and properly managed way. Some senior academic administrators even claim it is impossible. Discussions about retraining and redeployment too often stop at the theoretical level because universities have no systematic procedures for this type of transition. They may also underestimate the desirability of such changes for maintaining an academic environment in which faculty members are productive and feel a strong sense of accomplishment and collegiality.

The most obvious factor in migrating is that you would have to allow yourself a reasonable amount of time to catch up on where the field is at the present time, and where it will be when you overtake it. You won't have to read everything written over the past twenty years, because a lot will have been superseded anyway but it could nevertheless be important for developing a sense of history of where and how the present state of knowledge had its origins.

A point to be aware of is that a person may strike out in what appears to be a new and exciting direction, only to find later that this direction is not so much at the cutting edge of the field itself as just being new and exciting *to the person*. Researchers in the field may have grappled with the issues years ago, and resolved them to the point where further research no longer takes place.

I recently reviewed an article in my field where two authors claimed to have discovered a new method for gathering and validating data. Unfortunately for them, the approach had been developed about fifteen years earlier in another field and was described in several textbooks, including one on my shelves. Their literature search had failed for two reasons. First, it had been limited to the previous decade, which in this particular instance was not far enough back. Second, the new researchers had used their own terminology for the search. Although theirs made good intuitive sense, the original terminology had been different. So even if they had had the search period right, the terminology hurdle would have still blocked them.

These obstacles aside, migration from one field to another can, in the right circumstances, achieve excellent results. It is astonishing how many major advances in various disciplines have been made by people who have switched interests. They seem to have brought to their new area not only intensity and enthusiasm, but also a different set of lenses through which to view the progress to date and the challenges ahead.

You obviously enjoy academic life and have a lot to offer. I hope you can make the change that works best for you.

9

Coping with career interruptions

Dear Sarah,

Many academics have their careers interrupted, possibly for years at a time, by child rearing, caring for disabled relatives or aging parents, or having to resign from a position due to geographical relocation and being unable to find another one. Sometimes these discontinuities result from lifestyle decisions that academics make voluntarily, such as working for an extended period abroad, in industry or for a government agency. Others result from force of circumstances over which the person has no control. Whatever the reason, the reality of career breaks has to be factored into overall career development.

The general strategy should be to maximise the benefit from the active periods, and minimise the losses during breaks. The suggestions below cover both of these aspects.

CONCENTRATE ON ACTIVITIES THAT ARE HIGH-LEVERAGE

Some things count more than others for career advancement. It is therefore important to make room for high-priority activities at the expense of lower priority activities, and to be fairly hard-nosed about it. Universities differ in how they regard teaching, research and service, but many expect performance on all three.

STICK TO STRICT TIME MANAGEMENT PRINCIPLES

This means organising your office hours so that the time available is never wasted, but used productively. This doesn't mean cutting out social or academic contact with colleagues, just making sure time isn't frittered away unnecessarily. It also means placing limits on your involvement in committee work. Even the choice of committees is important. Some may have the potential for stretching your thinking in new directions, which may benefit your teaching or research. Others may meet too often, under a weak chair, and yield results that are not worth the time invested.

SET CLEAR, REALISTIC GOALS

Many universities expect that every faculty member should be an active researcher. Surveys of academics show that writing and research productivity is one of their primary professional concerns, in many cases their major one. They have difficulty finding time to do themselves justice on this front. The time they do have never seems to be enough, and is often fragmented because of unavoidable non-academic obligations. The aim should be to work at a moderate but sustainable pace over several years. Research productivity across academics, both females and males, varies widely. A small proportion produce most of the output, the majority produce relatively little output, and a considerable proportion produce none at all. A modest but consistent rate of production will, over time, pull an academic up at least into the higher productivity portion of the middle group.

The nature of the output can also be crucial to success. Unless special circumstances apply, a proportion of research activity should be in the primary discipline area. Some academics are appointed to a particular substantive post but then research exclusively in an associated area, such as the history, teaching, or gender aspects of the discipline. These areas are entirely appropriate for academics in whose field they constitute part of the mainstream and are a natural fit. In other fields, however, pursuing a second-order research agenda to the virtual exclusion of traditional substantive research may not count as much for career advancement.

AIM FOR PERIODIC CLOSURE ON KEY OBJECTIVES

Sometimes the timing and duration of career breaks can be anticipated in advance, sometimes not. If the career path is likely to proceed in discontinuous stages, it is important to have 'products' completed at each stage if at all possible. In teaching, the product may be a course that is developed, taught and evaluated. In research, it may be a journal article that is written, refereed and accepted for publication.

Most academic interests, including teaching and research-in-progress, simply cannot be carried forward and resumed after a substantial break. Typically, too many things change. A partly written monograph that seemed so full of promise at a particular time has a habit of either losing relevance or never getting finished once momentum is lost. So unless projects are conceptualised, sized appropriately, carried out, and wrapped up within the same career stage, it becomes very difficult later to demonstrate concrete attainments and achieve career progression.

MAINTAIN ACADEMIC INTERESTS DURING CAREER BREAKS

If at all possible, take steps to maintain and update your knowledge and skill base. You may be able to engage in some part-time teaching, or to act as a research assistant on an ongoing project where you can work flexible hours to fit in with your other commitments. Alternatively, you may be able to undertake advanced studies, possibly through flexible learning opportunities that are now widely available from a range of universities. Take advantage of modern communication technologies that allow you to work from home on data analysis, writing, editing and even carrying out certain types of research.

10

Confronting bias and discrimination

Dear Jasmin,

There are many things that can obstruct your progress as an academic. Some problems exist at the institutional level, some at departmental level, and others with individuals. Institutional cultures and ethos depend on a variety of factors, including the history of the organisation, the existence of policies on equity and justice, and whether the university has the determination to put policies into effect.

Bias or discrimination against a person occurs when a decision that affects that person is made for reasons other than those strictly relevant to the case. Bias can be either positive (the person is advantaged by comparison with others) or negative (the person is disadvantaged). The decision itself may be made by a single person, such as an academic supervisor, or by a committee overseeing such matters as the allocation of resources, research grants or special leave. It can also be made by colleagues. Discrimination occurs when a decision is influenced by factors other than those that are considered legitimate in the context. Positive discrimination can be justified in certain circumstances, but the conditions under which it is exercised must be made explicit and accepted by the academic community concerned.

The most troublesome form of discrimination is the negative kind, particularly when it is based on prejudice associated with gender, or cultural and ethnic stereotypes. It is often expressed in subtle ways that have to be experienced for them to be detected at all. This does not make them any less real, but it may make it difficult to convince others about them. If they were more overt or more widespread, they could be identified, classified, given a name and an attempt made to deal with them. But they often remain for years below the threshold of visibility. On the other hand, explicit policies, even if they do exist, do not necessarily have much impact if the culture of the organisation is, in essence, indifferent or hostile towards them, or if the policies are so weak they can easily be subverted.

I have three suggestions for dealing with bias at the personal level, that is, for achieving redress for an unfair decision.

MAKE AN ASSESSMENT OF THE SITUATION AS OBJECTIVELY AS POSSIBLE

Sometimes a person experiences an event that is negative and takes it personally as clear evidence of discrimination against them. An alternative explanation may, however, exist. People have their own distinctive ways of 'filling in' missing information. Optimists do it one way, pessimists another. It is important to reduce the probability of incorrectly attributing bias when it may not be a significant factor. Try to be objective when obtaining corroborative evidence about what the situation really is.

In one case I know of, two academics were being considered for tenure. One application was turned down, while that of an apparently equally qualified colleague succeeded. They both appeared to be competent teachers, and their research records were comparable. The unsuccessful applicant believed that discrimination on ethnic grounds was the reason, and appealed the decision. It turned out that the tenure committee had made its determination strictly on the evidence before it. Although the successful applicant's teaching was not brilliant, it was nevertheless satisfactory. The crucial factor was that teaching performance had been carefully documented and validating evidence produced. On the other hand, the other teaching submission consisted almost entirely of assertion and self-report. Although these claims may have been substantially correct, there was no corroborating evidence and the committee was unable to recommend tenure at that point.

Assuming that this particular rejection was based on prejudice was unhelpful in that it led to feelings of anger and frustration, and seriously affected this academic's confidence. These emotions then become additional problems to overcome. An important step is to check so far as you are able that discrimination has actually taken place.

MAKE USE OF THE INSTITUTION'S FORMAL COMPLAINT PROCEDURES

Get hold of a copy of the university's equity or equal employment opportunity policy, and prepare to work systematically through the procedures. Arrange to discuss your situation, informally in the first instance, with one of the officers designated to handle these issues. They are usually both approachable and knowledgeable about what to do. They can be relied on to know all the options, and are experienced in helping colleagues put the necessary information together. In addition, they can provide moral support so that you don't feel overwhelmed.

Complaints can only be made on clear, documented evidence, not on general impressions or hearsay. For this reason, it is important to keep accurate notes of dates, descriptions of unacceptable behaviour, or details of what has actually been said, verbatim if at all possible. Also keep a record of how these behaviours have affected you and your work. A complaint usually cannot proceed unless this sort of specific information is available.

KNOW HOW TO GET INFORMATION AND DEFEND YOURSELF

The blunt way to get information is to demand it, to stand up for your rights, and to exercise any legal options available. That is often an ineffective way as well, although it seems to immediately appeal to some people. Once you start down that road, procedures typically become rigidly legal, very quickly. To request, for example, every document in the university that has anything to do with your employment, confirmation, promotion or research support may in fact yield far more than you need, or would even care to see. In some cases, you could find out things that you would rather not have known, which may affect *your* attitude towards yourself or your colleagues. Besides, the university may take a considerable time to process such a request, and certain classes of documents, such as confidential referees' reports, may be legally protected and hence unavailable.

You need to be very pragmatic and take all aspects into consideration. At the same time, there are often good reasons why certain things need to be in writing. There are plenty of situations where a person requires specific information in permanent form so that it can be referred to later. The following strategy often works well, although it requires care and patience.

As a general rule, start at the level where the decision has been made, and work upward only as far as you need. The starting point may well be the person who made the decision, or the chair if a committee made it. Suppose it is the latter. If you immediately jump to the top level, say to the university's Chief Executive Officer, the matter will be referred straight down the institution's management line, perhaps through people in intermediate positions. Many more people then come to know about the situation, and this in turn could make the committee chair feel squeezed and defensive. You need the chair's maximum cooperation, because that is the most likely repository of all the critical information.

First talk to the committee chair. Explain that you are not satisfied with the decision, and that you want a written clarification so that you can plan for the future. Go through your key questions, being careful not to accuse people. Indicate that you will be making a formal written request for answers to those questions in the near future. Try to get the chair on side, but be aware that you are not likely to get confidential information about other faculty members no matter how subtly you ask. Ask the chair for some guidance on the kinds of questions you could reasonably expect answers to, and how best to word them.

Then draft a letter of request. Be quite specific about the things you need to know, and why. When you have finished the draft, label it as a DRAFT, leave it unsigned and send it to the chair. In a covering note, or perhaps in person, tell the chair that this is a draft of what you propose to submit. Ask them to go through it, to correct it for omissions or errors of fact, to advise you of any inappropriate assumptions you have made or questions that have no answer in the way they have been framed, and to suggest other ways to improve it. This step makes it difficult for the chair to later dismiss your request on technical grounds such as inaccuracy, but also keeps that person involved in the process. When you have finished the second version, sign it and forward it. In most cases, this will give you most of the information you need. In complex cases, it may be put to the whole committee for its consideration before a reply is written.

If you are faced with hostility or a refusal to cooperate, or consider that evasion or discrimination is still taking place, explain that you intend to take the matter further. To do this, move up one level within the university and basically repeat the process. The next level would normally be the body or person to whom the committee and its chair report.

In principle, you could work your way systematically through all the levels of the university if necessary. In practice, however, it may be wise to reassess the situation at each stage to see whether it is worth pursuing. You may simply decide to cut your losses and stop. It is possible for something like this to grow until it takes over your whole life. The information you seek may not even exist in the form you think it should. Then no amount of looking would find it, and there may well be more profitable things you could do with your time.

IN SPECIAL CIRCUMSTANCES

If bias seems to pervade the institution, and if you are a strong player, taking on the establishment over bias and discrimination can possibly be turned to positive career benefit. Academics who take up posts at the lower ranks typically lack both representation and power in the organisation. Unless a strong and articulate advocate in a position of authority takes up the cause, junior academics are left with the task of either doing it themselves or not at all. To work against the norm for the purpose of accelerating its transformation requires activism, argument, time, tact, negotiating skills, and passion for the task, if it is to be successful. A strong commitment to these activities, however, inevitably leaves less energy for teaching and research, which are generally regarded as core academic work. The dual task of contributing to changing the culture while at the same time pursuing a career in the 'standard' way places a significant burden on any academic who attempts it. Among other things, they need to be streetwise, able to cope with feelings of vulnerability, and able to hold at bay the sense that the institution is treating them unfairly.

Each of us has only so much discretionary time. It is important to sort out where you most want to make your contribution, and to allocate the time so as to achieve maximum long-term advantage.

Suppose that the academic culture of a university really needs to be shaken up and reformed, and that a particular person is suitably qualified to make a contribution. Several options may lie before them. On the one hand, they may decide that attending to their career is the top priority, and that they will work within the current norms and values to advance through the academic ranks. As they achieve respect and position within the institution, so they have increasing opportunity to influence policies and bring about change. Eventually they may also be able to serve as a role model and advocate for others. All this assumes that they maintain their original vision and don't become co-opted by the system they are trying to influence.

On the other hand, they may decide that reform is for the here and now, not for some time in the indefinite and uncertain future. Many academics who belong to minority or other special groups feel that they must, as a matter of principle, run with the dual agenda outlined earlier; that is, achieve in terms of academic performance and also on the anti-bias policy front. People who, because of their particular status, volunteer or are invited to be on departmental or university committees can easily find that the time commitments for these leave them little time for anything else. The smaller the size of the group of which they are a member, the greater the pressure, particularly if they have special expertise, are in high demand, enjoy doing it, and experience a strong sense of efficacy.

Work strategically and apportion energy according to priorities

Multiple committee memberships may certainly help to achieve changes in institutional policy and practice, but if too much time is devoted to them career objectives may be sacrificed. However valuable these contributions may be to the institution and to the cause, they may not be accepted in the institution as substitutes for achievements on other fronts.

Alternatives to multiple committee memberships exist. They involve creative thinking, and action on a different level and scale. The first step is to articulate what the issue or cause is by asking: Of what general *class* of problems in this university is mine a particular case? The next step is to scour the environment for other individuals or types of people whose specific situation may be different but whose problems fall within the same class. Identifying other people or groups allows the person who is taking the initiative to make strategic alliances with them and to share the load. The combined group can work towards getting the situation remedied in generic rather than narrow terms. The aims are to build solidarity with others who may suffer discrimination, to broaden the agenda to obtain greater exposure and impact, and to use resources to greatest advantage.

Put your achievements to career advantage

If a deliberate decision is made to follow this line of action as a priority, it is important not only to take account of the risks involved but also to realise that exceptional service in this regard will probably have to be portrayed and accepted as some compensation for achievements in other areas. You would have to maintain documentation of involvement and leadership in the process, including all successes along the way. This would be crucial in later demonstrating a strong commitment to social justice and service to the institution, or in seeking a position elsewhere.

Part two

APPLYING FOR JOBS AND PROMOTIONS

11

Compiling a curriculum vitae

Dear Suzy,

A curriculum vitae (CV) is vitally important for every academic to compile and maintain. Before I give you suggestions on what a CV should contain, I need to point out that, in some quarters, a clear distinction is made between a CV and what is called a résumé. A résumé is usually a summary document, shorter than a standard CV, and specifically tailored to be the key part of an application for a particular position. After a preliminary round of sifting the applications to identify the most promising ones, a selection panel may then request full CVs from those applicants who are on the short list. In some contexts, however, a résumé and a CV are regarded as synonymous. If you are in any doubt about terminology and the correct way to apply for a position, check with one of your senior colleagues or with the institution where the vacancy exists. My comments are really about a CV of the more comprehensive type.

What should be included in your CV? In broad terms,

all of those things that represent significant events, achievements or awards in your academic career to date. As a general rule, the various guides to résumé writing you see in regular bookshops will be of limited help in putting together an academic CV. Those books cater for a different audience.

Because you are still in the early stages of your academic career, you may not find it easy to gain access to a variety of CVs to see how they are typically put together. Although members of appointment and promotion committees routinely see a wide range of CVs, academics do not share their CVs among themselves much, unless there is a specific purpose. This can lead, among other things, to almost complete ignorance of what the academic in the office next door has actually achieved. A person's research achievements are often better known to colleagues in another university than to the people they see every day.

The typical CV will include:

- Relevant personal details, such as your full name, home address, contact details (including e-mail address and facsimile number), nationality, and residency status (if not a citizen of the country you live in). Some things are optional here, such as marital status, age, gender, and family dependants. Frequently nowadays, many of these are omitted.

- Key aspects of your education. Concentrate on your post-school studies, but include a short reference to any outstanding achievement or honour (such as School Captain) at school. List diplomas and degrees awarded and the field of specialisation if it is relevant, especially for advanced degrees. Including the titles of any dissertations completed is often useful.

- A summary of your employment history, including the position titles, length of service in each, and levels of appointment within those, including any promotions or honours.

- Details of significant memberships of statutory authorities, key university committees, scholarly or professional associations, external boards or commissions, and government inquiries or reviews; an outline of your participation in major consultancies.
- Details of your teaching responsibilities in your current position, with earlier teaching information if it is relevant.
- Details of research higher degrees successfully supervised to conclusion, and brief details of Honours and research higher degree students currently being supervised and whether you are the sole, principal or co-supervisor.
- List of formal publications and conference papers presented. This section is of major importance for academic appointments that have a research component, because your previous record is taken as a clear indication of future potential. Grouping similar research outputs together is widely practised, and strongly recommended. Thus, you might put books first (authored, then edited), refereed journal articles, book chapters, other articles (say, non-refereed or in professional publications) and then conference papers. If the last mentioned are published in formal proceedings, possibly after peer review, they should in most cases be included. Other conference papers are often omitted altogether because of the variable quality control, or listed only if they are from the last two years. The order in which items are listed within classes is often reverse chronological, with the most recent first. Straight chronological is also common.

That probably seems like a long list, and you may have only a little to put into some of the categories. Don't worry about that at all. Leave a category out altogether if you have to. The order of listing typically follows that above, but in some departments the CV takes a standardised form and is kept on file for reference. In this case, you should get hold of the preferred form.

Now for a few comments about CVs in general. First, a CV should be kept up to date. Many academics update theirs as soon as any change occurs in their publication records, which may be as often as six times a year. A common format for publications is: author, date, title of the work, and publication details. This is much the same in principle as for many academic journals. A manuscript that has been submitted to a journal but is still waiting on an editorial decision should be listed in a separate section under 'Work in progress', not as a publication. In the period between firm acceptance by a journal and formal publication, list the item with the publications proper, with the words 'in press' replacing the date.

Second, be careful not to appear to be double counting. For example, a paper that appeared first as a working document, was later delivered at a conference, then included in the proceedings, and was ultimately published as a journal article might not deserve four entries. But republication, for example in an Annual Review of the discipline, definitely deserves double listing if the article has been selected as representative of the best publications in the field during the review period.

Third, keep the entries in your CV consistent with respect to career significance. If you try to be too comprehensive, you may flood the really important material with trivial detail, making the former harder to identify. A CV is evaluated not only for what it contains (the substance) but also as a document that indicates the person's ability to use discretion and good judgment.

Fourth, from your master CV tailor different versions as required to suit various purposes, such as applying for different positions. These versions will vary in length, detail and emphasis, but would be easily recognised as different versions of the same CV. It is also useful to have a very truncated CV, sometimes called biodata, to produce on demand for publicity purposes for a flyer or for a journal's 'Notes about the Contributors'.

Fifth, the standard of presentation matters, but will not make up for substance. Some books on résumé writing make it sound as if presentation is everything: shop around for the very best paper, use plenty of white space, dress up the layout by having the CV professionally prepared, and so on. I have yet to find a university committee that thought any of this was a great idea, although it may sway opinion elsewhere. Professional résumé writers don't necessarily understand the expectations of universities, and overemphasise presentation. The result is often a CV that has two or three times as many pages as it should have, with fancy designs and layout. It may actually be counterproductive. Remember that during the selection processes in universities, up to fifteen copies of a CV may be made. It helps if they include everything that matters but are not inordinately long.

Finally, there is a sense in which a CV's form and content should 'mature' over successive stages of a career. Matters that are salient early in one's career may be almost irrelevant later on, and can therefore safely be excluded. Some will always remain legitimate and important items for the record. Try to keep your CV down to a reasonable length, say six to eight pages. This means that as your career progresses you will have to cull your CV systematically so that it always remains a reflection of your most significant achievements. In any case, most readers of CVs understand that significant achievements at one point in a career are often the result of a series of related achievements earlier on, so it may not be necessary for these to be separately listed.

Once you have what you think is a reasonable draft of your own CV, approach three or four colleagues, including at least one of more senior rank, to exchange and discuss CVs.

12

Developing a label for your career

Dear Tami,

It is regrettable that you and a lot of other highly qualified people have been forced to accept a string of short-term appointments, many of them for only a year at a time. At least you have been able to find some openings, even if none has been long-term so far. Unfortunately, many excellent PhD-holders cannot find any academic vacancies in their fields at all.

Given the uncertainty of continuation from year to year in the current climate, the major problem of one-year appointments is that you have to start looking around for another position only six months into taking it up, as you know only too well. That splits your available energy. The job-hunting side simply has to be taken seriously, giving you less time for your students and your research. In turn, this sets up a negative spiral that can be hard to break out of at the very time that you should, in theory, be concentrating on establishing your academic credentials further.

Having come out of a professional field into the academic world, it would certainly be good if your job security and future prospects appeared as bright as they did in your previous position. Although it will not be easy, you do have to adapt to the environment. It will be hard to maintain your sense of optimism and confidence without becoming bitter and cynical. I am not telling you anything you don't already know, I'm sure.

This is an incident that occurred a few years ago. I was a member of a selection committee and we were interviewing the short-listed candidates for a two-year contract position. A very senior member of the university said something like this to one of the candidates: 'Looking through your application, your career comes over as a bit of hotchpotch. You seem to lurch from one field to another, and one position to another, and don't seem to have settled down in nearly a decade to a career pattern with a coherent research program.'

It wasn't said unkindly, and I could see the point being made. But in this instance it was totally unfair. For various personal reasons, this applicant's work had to be in one of the three major universities in a capital city, and she essentially had to take up whatever positions she could get. This led to a series of short-term contracts, the longest being three years, in various branches of the discipline.

The candidate seemed a bit shaken by the question and its implications. She then responded by saying that she had had difficulty establishing anything like a research profile. No sooner would she begin research with colleagues in one of the universities when that contract would run out. She would then be on the job market again, having to take whatever came up.

Later on, I did some more thinking about this candidate's situation. I looked at the various contract positions she had held over the previous years. She had been, in turn: a faculty member teaching courses in special education; an administrative officer in the student affairs office of a university, where she was responsible for special entry procedures for university applicants who lacked standard academic qualifications; a teacher in adult literacy at a higher education institution; a study skills coordinator for university students in their first year; and a senior research assistant in a centre for ethics and public policy. Despite the apparent differences between these positions, they could all be interpreted as being elements of a larger whole. This whole could be seen as a sort of envelope into which the various employment episodes could be placed and a meaningful label attached. A lot hinged on finding the best label. In her case, all of the positions and the work she had done in them were related to 'access and equity'. In other words, if one took a broader, retrospective view of how her collection of appointments could be described, it is possible to reconceptualise what she had already done and achieved, and see it all not as unrelated bits but as varieties of a whole. When I mentioned this to her, she agreed that the access and equity issue was really where her heart lay. I have since talked this idea through with a number of other colleagues in similar situations who said they found it helpful.

You have heard me talk in seminars about the necessity of having a clear research focus. In case you are thinking that what I have just said contradicts this, I see the two situations as different. What I am suggesting to you here is the idea of casting some meaningful terms around what may appear to others to be disjointed employment experiences. This would be essentially for your own benefit but could also serve as an explanatory device from time to time. It also does not necessarily have much to do with ambition as such, but with clarifying your own vision and feeling less fragmented.

I don't claim any originality for the strategy. Companies have to do this sort of thing from time to time to stay in business and prosper. Otherwise they find they can get fixated on their traditional line of business, such as manufacturing something, or providing a particular type of service. When external circumstances change, specifically their markets, they have to either adapt or decline. A powerful adaptation strategy is to ask a fairly simple set of related questions: What is the *essential* nature of the business we are in? Of what general enterprise is ours a particular case? How should we reconceptualise what we are doing, to our advantage? The difference between hamburgers (as the particular) and fast foods (as the general) illustrates this difference in specificity.

Maybe you could look back over your last eight years to see if you can identify common elements, regardless of the actual job titles. Try to come up with an appropriate encompassing label, a theme that seems to run through most of your short-term contracts so that you view them as a totality rather than as distinctly different. It might even help if you happen to get a 'career' question at an interview for a future position. The aim should be to develop a sense of career out of what to date has been a sequence of jobs.

I don't see this idea of developing a career label as at all pretentious. It can be quite enabling. It has to do at least in part with where you want to head in the longer term, not only or necessarily in terms of particular academic positions, but also in terms of a general orientation towards an academic interest and research area that you feel could keep you excited and productive for, say, a five-year stretch.

For that to work, you would have to experiment with developing research interests and styles that provide you with a reasonable degree of portability and continuity across jobs. That is probably worth some thought as well.

13

Choosing academic referees

Dear Briony,

Yes, I am prepared to act as one of your referees for the position being advertised, but to be quite frank I have some reservations. You might be better nominating someone who knows your teaching, research and administrative work more intimately than I do. My reservations, therefore, are not about you personally or your ability to do the job well. They are about my ability to do justice to you. You need referees who can speak authoritatively about you and on your behalf.

I could certainly provide something like a character reference, and also my recollections of you as an Honours student and later as a short-term colleague. But all of that was a long time ago. I could not say I have any first-hand (or even second-hand) experience of your recent work in the three areas specifically listed in the duty statement: teaching performance, research and scholarship, and academic leadership. So your request places me in a difficult position. On the one hand, I would like to see you progress in an academic career. You have always shown great promise. I also value your friendship. On the other hand, I am limited in what I could say that would be useful to a selection committee. It would be no good my making things up, or trying to project myself into your present context.

You said that if I agreed, you would send me copies of the advertisement, the position description, your application and your CV. I would certainly need all of these. You would be surprised how many job applicants don't do that. Maybe they assume that the secretary of the selection committee will provide them when requesting the confidential reference. Sometimes that does happen, but often the attachments to the request are limited to copies of the advertisement, the duty statement and the selection criteria. The referee then has to either contact the applicant, which causes delay, or guess what was probably in the application, and thereby run some risks.

Even if you did send me all the relevant details, what would you be hoping I would do with the information? The committee members will read your résumé and CV carefully, so there would not be a lot of point in my reiterating material these documents already contain. I could perhaps comment on whether I think your achievements would be relevant to the position, but that is really the job of the selection committee itself. In making a judgment on that, they would be influenced by the size and nature of the field of applicants that the advertisement draws, and the committee's intimate knowledge of the position to be filled. They will simply want to appoint the best candidate. If none is suitable, they might wait a while, then readvertise to see if they draw a different or more extensive set of applications.

Referees are usually expected to go beyond what the candidate puts forward in the application, and provide confidential relevant information that is NOT in the application! An exception to this is when the committee itself arranges for an external expert to provide a comparative referee's report based essentially on the material contained in the applications of the front-runners. But this seems to happen only for senior positions, when it happens at all.

You asked me in passing if the status of the referees matters. Well, it does and it doesn't. Generally, the higher the academic rank of the referee the better, but relevance and knowledge about the candidate should not be sacrificed to mere rank. I have read references that could be paraphrased more or less as follows: 'I knew this person years ago, but have actually had very little contact since. The person seemed to be very bright, was committed to good teaching, and had a pleasant, outgoing personality. I don't really have any up-to-date knowledge about current performance or achievements.' End of story.

That type of reference is unhelpful to both the candidate and the selection committee, and could actually do damage. Committee members would probably ask themselves: Why did the applicant nominate this particular referee at all?

One factor that should influence the rank of the referees nominated is the level of the position being applied for. If it is for an associate professorship, drawing all referees from a lower rank will not cut much ice with the committee. In fact, at least one and possibly more should be a full professor. Certainly, the person you report to academically should be listed. Otherwise, the committee will wonder what there is to hide, and may contact this person anyway, if this is allowed for under the institution's protocols. If you have changed positions recently, your previous supervisor might also be highly appropriate. In these cases, the role relationship is more significant than academic seniority.

You should also choose referees who complement one another with respect to your application. One of them might be able to speak knowledgeably about your teaching, another about your research work, and another about administrative and professional service or more general academic matters. If you do have this targeting in mind, be sure to let the referees know your reason for listing them and the perspective from which you would like them to speak.

One more thing: not every word that every referee writes will necessarily be enthusiastically favourable. Selection committees are suspicious about galaxy-shattering prose, and they are naturally suspicious about those sorts of reports. The committee looks for a balanced assessment, and knows that not everyone is perfect, or has achieved brilliantly on all fronts. The selection criteria are ideals, and even if no candidate meets all of them to an outstanding degree, several candidates may still be highly appointable.

What all this amounts to is that any person likely to apply for a position in the not-too-distant future should give thought not only to their qualifications, experience and achievements but also to strategies that make for effective applications. Among other things, this means giving thought to potential referees, and in a sense nurturing them. I don't mean buttering them up, but simply keeping them informed of your career as it develops, and keeping in touch. That way, they are likely to feel more knowledgeable about you, and therefore more confident in writing a reference that means something.

You mentioned that the position advertised seems as if it has been designed specifically for you, because this is the type of work you really want to do and you clearly satisfy all of the selection criteria. You say that provided your application is received on time, you should certainly make it to the interview stage at least. This definitely suggests a good fit with your qualifications and experience, and I hope you are shortlisted.

If things turn out differently, however, you should not feel devastated. What neither you nor I know, and most probably will never know, is the strength of the field of candidates who will apply for this vacancy. Some of the applicants could well be international, and the amount of competition is difficult to predict. Suppose an exceptionally strong set of applications is received, and that there are at least fifteen applicants whose qualifications and experience are far in excess of what the university reasonably expected when it drafted the advertisement. Included in these, let's say, are some simply dazzling applications. The limited number of candidates whose referees would be contacted, and the presumably smaller number again selected for interview, would be the truly outstanding candidates. This type of sifting process is quite normal, but it does mean that many well-qualified applicants do not get anywhere near the interview stage. I mention this so that, in the event that you are not interviewed, you don't presume that your application was weak, that you did not satisfy all of the criteria, or that the university's procedures were biased or faulty.

I leave the next move to you. If you still want to include my name as a referee, I will certainly do what I can. I really hope you get the job. If you don't, maybe something in this letter might be helpful for the future.

14

Assessing promotional prospects

Dear Bharat,

Having taken up an academic appointment after years of industry experience, it is only natural for you to feel you have a lot of catching up to do to establish yourself as an academic. It is also quite natural that you should be exploring what your prospects might be for advancement in the new environment.

The professional experience you have had to date will, without a doubt, continue to pay dividends in your teaching and research. Lots of academics have never left the university setting to get working experience outside, including some who work in professional departments. Many of these would give anything to have current hands-on experience as a practitioner. The cost of doing it at their career stage is, they figure, just too high. So instead of feeling that you may have 'wasted' time, look at that experience as a resource that you will be able to tap into for years ahead.

You asked specifically about how I evaluate your promotional prospects, and what I think of several alternatives. I will begin with the issue of promotion.

In an important sense, different criteria are applied for appointment from outside the university to a vacancy carrying a particular academic rank, compared with the criteria for promotion within the institution to that same academic rank. On the surface, you might think that they should be identical, and that this should be the minimum condition for fairness. In practice, though, things are a lot more fluid and complicated. The criteria are not necessarily the same. In the event that they are technically the same, they may well be weighted differently. The reasons lie in the circumstances. It is therefore impossible to generalise and say, for example, that it is 'easier' to be appointed to a higher level at another university than to be promoted in your own institution. The reverse may well apply. Some hypothetical examples will help to flesh this out a bit.

Consider first a professional department such as the one you are in. Most of the teaching is directed towards preparing students for a career in a reasonably well-defined field. In such cases, the graduates often have to be externally accredited by some sort of registration or licensing board before they can practise legally. A common arrangement is for the university program itself to be accredited by the licensing authority, which cooperates with the institution to develop satisfactory program content and structure. Graduates are then automatically eligible for registration. For some professions, the agency sets its own examinations independently. I will ignore those for this illustration.

In the case of these accredited programs, there may be a clear need for the teaching or clinical department to make appointments in specific disciplinary or professional areas. Depending on departmental policy and expectations, there may be strong preference for a person with recent, relevant professional experience. This is perfectly understandable. Clearly, if a position is to be filled in this way, the vacancy has to be advertised with conditions that will make it attractive to practising professionals who are adequately qualified.

Suppose an appointment simply *must* be made for accreditation purposes. If at least one applicant is technically appointable, it is reasonable for the department to go ahead with an offer. The overriding consideration under those circumstances is to hire the best person available from among the qualified applicants. In this situation, the actual criteria for appointment could justifiably be different from the standard criteria for promotion.

Let me take this one step further. If the component of the accredited program is substantial, at least one faculty position will probably need to be at a relatively senior academic level to provide suitable leadership. An advertisement at a relatively junior level, which may be the norm for filling routine vacancies in the university, may in this instance draw a very small field of applications. Perhaps nobody at all would be appointable. By contrast, advertising at a senior level would draw a strong field.

I have cast the above scenario in terms of professional accreditation. Much the same applies when a particular niche has to be filled in a research team, or when a new profession emerges and develops quickly as a result of advances in technology or societal demand. If practically all the experts in a field are already professionally engaged, and perhaps paid handsome salaries, it may be hard to entice some of them into the academic arena where conditions of employment may be less attractive. In these situations, the criteria for appointment are obviously affected by supply and demand.

By contrast, when applications for promotion are being considered within the department or within the university, often less account needs to be taken of external considerations. Applicants for promotion are more likely to be evaluated against the criteria and standards laid down in university policy documents. One of the aims is to achieve consistency in decision making in comparison with other applicants for promotion in the same broad area within the university.

When the number of available internal promotions is rigidly controlled, supply and demand again play a crucial role. The strength of each applicant's case is compared with the strengths of other cases, and the standards are likely to vary somewhat from year to year. In a fiercely competitive environment, the expectations of promotion committees may appear to, and often actually do, escalate steadily each year. This can lead more recent appointees to the university to feel they have no way of ever making the grade.

There is another aspect to this issue that is often misunderstood. I have known cases in which a person practising as a successful professional has exchanged this for a middle-ranking position in a university, but has then run into difficulties when seeking further promotion. From what I have outlined above, you can see why. An application for further promotion immediately invokes the standard internal promotion criteria, with firm expectations about teaching and research performance. Professional experience may still be important, but might not be as highly valued as for the initial appointment.

The second issue you mentioned, namely whether you should forego all thought of promotion but increase your income by book royalties and private consultancies, is something that you should weigh up carefully. The possibility of book royalties might sound attractive, but don't hold your breath waiting for the revenue to flood in. Unless you write, say, a very successful first-year textbook with substantial adoptions and large student numbers, the net proceeds are likely to be rather slim. Do some exploration as to what the competing books in the field are, for a start. See how firmly established they are before putting too much effort into this area. You never know; with your creative energy and extensive field experience you might produce a real winner.

If you do perceive a real need, then be sure to read up on the best way to go about publishing books, specifically textbooks, and make early contact with potential publishers. They can work with you in developing both the manuscript and the market for a successful release.

If, on the other hand, you are thinking of books that are of a more scholarly nature, including handbooks and specialist reference books, you might be surprised to find out how little disposable income they actually generate for authors. You could probably earn some pocket money, but not enough to supplement your current income substantially. In any case, recent publishing trends are for books to have a fairly short life actually in print. The initial print run is available for purchase by libraries, academics, professionals and anybody else. It is then remaindered. The days when publishers took pride in keeping books in print by maintaining stocks for a decade are well and truly over. A book has to continue to make a satisfactory profit or it is removed from the list.

Private consultancies are a different matter. You are in a quite special position in this regard. Although some academics in certain fields (such as the health and helping professions, law and business) may have retained the right to private practice as part of their terms of appointment, a host of other academics have virtually no opportunity to engage in either private practice or external consultancies.

In general, unless faculty members who have consultancies as a possible career option have already established external reputations and expertise, it is often difficult to lift consultancy programs off the ground. This is especially so if academics are to discharge their responsibilities to their employing universities fully. I realise that you presently have a lot of professional contacts as a result of your period in business and industry. Are these people in positions of authority? Do they have the power to commit funds? Sometimes 'understandings' are reached that simply cannot be honoured, despite all the goodwill in the world.

Furthermore, a lot of energy can go into developing the consultancies themselves unless you work in a lucrative area of high demand. Overheads and bidding processes consume resources, and normally only a handful of successful projects provide an economic yield. So in the first period of developing a consultancy program, there is a fair bit of front-end investment with not much return. Nevertheless, it is an option available to you, at least while your university rules permit it in the form you envision. Those rules can change. In the future, universities may tighten up their consultancy conditions, or place substantial levies on the income generated through them.

To return to the promotion issue, faculty members who consistently invest energy in developing expertise as a university teacher and in creating a record of significant publications in the field will almost always set themselves up well for promotion. If at some point later in your career you wish to consider an academic appointment in another university, a list of consultancies successfully completed may not carry nearly as much weight with an appointment committee as a commitment to teaching excellence and a reasonable research profile, particularly if you decide not to complete your doctorate.

Do some calculations. What would be your expected salary yield between next year and when you expect to retire if you were to be promoted to the next rank? How would this compare with a realistic estimate of what you could earn through royalties and consultancies? You might be surprised.

The blunt economics of it is only half the story. What really matters is working at the things that you enjoy, and that give you a sense of accomplishment and satisfaction.

15

Positioning for promotion

Dear Kim,

I am not surprised that a colleague has suggested that you should apply for promotion after only three years in your present position. Your work is obviously appreciated.

I have read through the copy of your CV, and can't help noticing that you have been extremely busy. However, as a 'second opinion', mine will inevitably be somewhat out of context. Although I know quite a few members of your department personally, I do not have much of a feel for how your promotion criteria are interpreted, or of the university culture in which decisions are made. I suggest you confide in a senior colleague with experience on a promotion committee to see whether you have a sustainable case in terms of your own institution's criteria and standards. You would not be bound by that opinion, but it is sometimes difficult for a person who is relatively new to academia to develop a sense for what is a sufficiently high standard. I will nevertheless provide below an outline of my perception of promotion procedures generally, together with some specific observations on your CV and what I know of your activities.

I fully agree that it is useful to consider readiness for promotion. Some academics seem to think that no one is ever successful in their first application, and that it always takes two, three or more attempts to get promoted. They seem to think that success comes primarily by wearing the committee down. I don't feel at all comfortable with that philosophy. I am not convinced that luck and brute persistence play much of a part.

There is a lot to be said for getting the timing right. Preparing and documenting a thorough application always requires a lot of energy, both mental and physical. It therefore takes time away from other activities, particularly research and writing. Applying before the case is strong sets a person up for disappointment. The applicant can become quite disheartened, frustrated or angry. A positive side, though, is that putting an application together forces a person to review their achievements. It can provide an incentive to take stock of where they currently are, and where they might go.

In your case, you have a three-year period to reflect on. Preparing a promotion application might provide you with experience in evaluating your career position systematically. If an interview with the promotion committee is involved, and this is the best or only way you can obtain reliable feedback, the exercise may prove useful on those grounds. But in general, the time and emotion that go into preparing a serious promotion application have to be evaluated in terms of a worthwhile investment in probable success.

A first step would be to check with your personnel officer that there is no technical barrier to your applying in the current round. Some universities have strict rules about eligibility for promotion. In particular, only persons at the top of their current salary classification may be eligible. Depending on your original level of appointment, that may have relevance for you. Other universities are less strict about this sort of thing, and will even permit a faculty member to jump a complete academic rank. Also check whether the university has any restrictions on how frequently a person may apply. Some place a two-year moratorium on re-application.

For promotion to be successful, there first of all has to *be* a case, then the applicant has to *make* the case. Either of these without the other is not likely to be successful. There must be substantial achievements, clearly satisfying the minimal threshold for promotion to the next academic rank. The strongest case is not necessarily made by a long application. If you decide to go ahead, confine your attention to developing one that is well organised, cogently and concisely written, and presented in an objective and well-crafted style. Having unambiguous and relevant evidence to support your claims is vitally important.

I notice that you are a member of five departmental committees, including the Academic Development Committee and Finance Committee. That you were elected by your colleagues to three of those, and appointed by the Dean to the other two, shows their confidence in your ability. I also note that you have coordinated both the first two years of a degree program, and the department's Learning Assistance Program for students needing help with university study. You are clearly recognised as an organiser, manager and administrator within the department, a bit of a mover and shaker.

You mentioned in your letter that other more senior persons in the department often seem to lack much gift or drive for administration. They don't contribute even half what you do to the department's smooth running and success. In your case, the big question is whether these substantial contributions are the kinds of achievements the promotion committee will give sufficient weight to.

You are recognised as a competent teacher, but your high performance in this area does not seem to me adequately supported, at least in the materials you sent. There are many ways of documenting excellence in teaching, including student evaluations, properly organised peer reviews, and reflective teaching portfolios. Some excellent guidelines for these have been published in the literature on university teaching. However, merely listing the curriculum development and program design you have been involved with to date, together with the actual courses taught, indicates only the scope of your activities, not necessarily their quality. If you were to make a bid for promotion on the basis of excellence in teaching, the committee would be looking for substantiation of any statements you make about your own teaching, even though they may all be quite true.

Your research output appears fairly thin from the point of view of scholarship. I note the policy documents you have produced within the department, and your contribution to two government reports, as well as your membership of a review committee for a research organisation. But in terms of peer-reviewed scholarship, such as articles in refereed journals, or even a small manuscript that has been reviewed by peers, your CV would need strengthening if you were at my university.

Contributions on the administrative side do not seem to carry as much weight as contributions to research and teaching, despite the fact that the department, and indeed students, have relied so heavily on your expertise and energy. I am all for generosity as a basic principle. But in your particular case, it may be necessary to be somewhat less generous in your availability at this stage in your career. You could find that your ability and willingness are being exploited. No matter how much administration you undertake, you need to have a balanced profile as a faculty member. The pressing need seems to me that you devote more of your efforts to documenting the quality of your teaching, and launching and pursuing your research interests.

You should be able to find out within your department the extent to which research productivity, excellence in teaching, and service to the faculty and the profession, can be traded against one another. In many university contexts, some compensations are possible. Nevertheless, minimum threshold levels for all three often do exist.

If you do decide to make a bid, allow yourself enough time to do it properly. There is no sense applying for promotion then finding out that it was a fruitless exercise from the start. Maybe next year?

16

Learning after non-promotion

Dear Melinda,

I sympathise with how disappointed you feel at not being promoted in this round. I know you are convinced that an injustice has been done. Maybe it has.

My experience, however, has been that all parties involved in the promotion process consider things very carefully, especially in the light of the appeals provisions. Committees weigh up the relative merits of different profiles of performance, along with the referees' reports. If, for example, one of four referees provided a particularly negative report, and the other three were highly positive, the committee would ordinarily investigate this discrepancy. There may or may not be a valid explanation. By and large, committees try to test the evidence and do not automatically take everything at face value.

I know you think it was discourteous of your head of department not to immediately telephone you with the bad news or deliver it personally. I don't know what was behind the situation in your case, but there may be a reason for it.

For example, I know of one head who decided to send the notifications through the normal internal mail channel in the first instance, because some faculty members had in the past found it very stressful to have to cope with the implications of a negative outcome in the personal presence of their head. They felt stunned, humiliated, distraught, and didn't know what to say. I suppose others would have liked someone to commiserate with immediately. It is a difficult time for all parties. Your head probably deserves the benefit of the doubt, even if the approach turned out to be the wrong one for you.

One of the difficulties with many promotional systems is that the applications of both successful and unsuccessful candidates are kept confidential by promotion committees, for obvious reasons. This makes it difficult for unsuccessful applicants to be able to see the full context in which decisions were made about their own cases. In particular, it makes it hard to find out exactly how one applicant stacked up against everyone else.

If I understand you correctly, the only feedback you seemed to get from the committee was that your record of research is below par. At the same time, your point is that one of the other candidates, whose research record is actually less significant than yours, was promoted. This does appear on the surface to be irregular. However, bear in mind that people often make assumptions about the research profiles of colleagues without knowing in concrete terms what those profiles are. Unless you have actually seen their applications and their current CVs, the strength of their cases would be hard to assess. Things aren't always what they seem.

I have been surprised on occasion to find that even strong advocates of research within a department, people who always seem to have many projects on the go at once and who are members of the research committee, are not necessarily high producers themselves. Occasionally, their research outputs are dismal. Conversely, colleagues who take a very low profile within a department may enjoy national and international reputations because of the excellence of their research publications, although this may not be widely known or appreciated among their immediate colleagues. These are extreme examples. Obviously I have no independent information about your context.

The other applicant you refer to, the one who *was* successful this time, may have had outstanding achievements in other areas of academic work, such as teaching. Again, this may not be highly visible to other members of the department. The selection committee, having all of the evidence before it, may have seen some of that outstanding achievement as partly compensating for what may seem to you a mediocre research record. That may not be at all inconsistent with the committee's feedback that, in your case, the research record itself is the area that needs strengthening.

What you naturally want to know is how the committee came to its decision. Your suggestion of getting extracts from the committee's minutes just might be helpful. However, most of the actual deliberations are unlikely to have been recorded, although the justification for the final recommendations almost certainly would have. You can usually get much more useful information off the record than you could by going straight for the official files. I suggest you contact the chair of the promotion committee and try to arrange a frank discussion about the aspects of your own performance, and perhaps the application itself, that need to be improved. What you might find unsatisfactory in such a discussion is the chair's reluctance to discuss with you other particular cases (specifically, the other applicants, successful or unsuccessful) for reasons of confidentiality. The chair might even appear a bit cagey in face-to-face discussion. You may have to settle for an explanation in quite general terms.

Here is another approach. Do you know any of the successful applicants reasonably well? Would they be open to a suggestion that the two of you talk over their successful experience, including a discussion of the actual application documents?

There is one more possibility. Because the promotion committees in your university operate across several related departments, you may know someone from another department who has just been promoted. Talking things over with a colleague at a little distance might be less daunting. Seeing one or two successful applications is certain to be helpful, although neither you nor the other candidates will ever know how far over the line they were. They might have romped in, or just squeaked home.

You mentioned the option of applying for every vacancy that comes up elsewhere as an alternative to trying to get promoted where you are. That may work for you, but can have a down side. First, you would have to nominate three or four academic referees for each application you make. Many institutions call for referees' reports only after the short-listing has been completed, while others send for the referees' reports for every applicant. Unless you have an extensive list of appropriate and willing referees, you would very quickly wear out the ones you have. They wouldn't take kindly to churning out one confidential reference after another, especially if you expected them to tailor an individual report for each position.

Second, suppose you were successful in being shortlisted for several positions. Would you really be prepared to accept each job if it were offered? You could reasonably expect an interviewing panel to ask whether you would definitely accept the position if a formal offer were made. An increasing number of selection committees now ask this question to test how serious a candidate really is. Unless you could give an unequivocal response, the committee may decline.

The reasons for the question may be several. Some academics think that if they apply for everything going, success will come sooner or later. They see job hunting as some sort of lottery. But word can get around. A committee may read scatter-gun applications as a signal that a person is desperate to escape from their present situation, and wonder why.

Other applicants apply for positions elsewhere so they can gain leverage for advancement in their own institutions. The theory goes like this. They apply for advancement and are unsuccessful. If another university offers them a more senior position, they then consider themselves hot property. Armed with this external assessment, they then re-approach the home institution to see if they can negotiate a better deal. Occasionally they can. Mostly, the home university will simply not be interested. Again, there could be several reasons for this. The university might want to discourage it as a regular practice because it is so time consuming and expensive for all concerned. Second, the university might then have to re-examine all other promotion decisions made at the same time. Finally, the university might simply adopt the attitude that no one is really irreplaceable. If the leverage doesn't work on the home ground, the attempt may nevertheless leave behind a negative residue which affects future opportunities. Anyone going for the leverage strategy has to be pretty sure of their ground.

On the other hand, a person who is made a significantly better offer elsewhere, and would definitely accept it, could find that their home institution approaches them with an attractive counter offer. This situation is quite different, in that the initiative lies with the home university. It is better to be choosy, and apply only for those positions where the type of work suits your qualifications and your experience, and which you would be prepared to accept if an offer were made.

I hope this fills in the picture to some extent, and that you have better success next time.

Part three

TEACHING

17

Helping students learn

Dear Sandy,

Your experience with students who simply do not improve in their work is similar to mine. Many university teachers who assess their students using a lot of written work also find the same thing. A lot of our satisfaction as teachers comes from seeing students grow. Yet when we look at the records of the students' achievements, the similarity between grades for their first and second term papers are uncanny. Some students get a little better, most seem to stay the same, and a few even seem to go backwards. What is going on? Naturally, we all want to see a better result.

In a sense, we do expect to see a certain consistency in performance. The more able students, however we judge that, are likely to produce superior work time after time, and the less able generally continue to produce mediocre work. So why don't we just accept that?

I am sure our concern is not simply that students seem to stay in the same relative positions through a sequence of tests.

It lies instead in what we believe to be rectifiable weaknesses in their work. No one would deny that writing extensive comments on student scripts is labour-intensive. Despite our best efforts, however, many of our students hand in work for later assignments with exactly the same deficiencies as in the earlier ones. Given the apparently singular ineffectiveness of the feedback we give, it's no wonder we experience a sense of impotence. We do everything we can to help students improve, but they don't—or won't—take us up on it.

Part of the solution may lie in having a better under-standing of the attitudes of students and the factors that are common to many university learning environments. There are a number of possibilities, four of which are outlined below

The first possibility is that the students really are improv-ing throughout the term, but that our expectations of them are being progressively raised at the same rate. This would effectively mask any real improvement. Comparing actual scripts from different points in the teaching term or from consecutive terms, preferably with our original feedback, would settle this one.

The second possibility is that some students are simply not interested or motivated to improve their performance. They set their sights on getting a passing grade, and are satisfied to submit work that they themselves realise is not of a very high standard. Some students know quite well how to produce high quality work, but given the availability of time and the nature of their other commitments, they choose not to. Each course they enrol in is worth a fixed amount of energy and that's it. A student once told me precisely that. The course I taught was not important enough in the big scheme of things to be worth a lot of effort. Performance in other courses showed that this student was capable of doing first-class work any time the need arose.

The third possibility is that some students may be actually incapable of producing better work. They work for all assignments at about their academic limit. It seems hard to believe, though, in an absolute ceiling effect in which the ceiling won't budge at all.

The fourth possible explanation is also the one that bothers me most as a teacher. It relates directly to the business of students who do not take on board the feedback from one assignment to improve performance on later assignments. What explains this apparent unwillingness or inability? Why doesn't feedback seem to transfer from one task to the next? Here are some of my thoughts on this.

Suppose that a student is given written criticism on an assignment. Even though both the student's original text and the criticism are placed before the student together, the meaning and significance of the feedback may not be apparent to the student. Let us assume that the flaw is due to the student's lack of appreciation of what the criticism implies, and not to a simple oversight or other lapse. In this situation, the student is in possession of a negative instance (their own defective text) and a negative appraisal (the grade itself and the instructor's comments), but has no corresponding positive instance or example that could either serve as a model or clarify what the feedback means. The connection between the feedback and the negative instance could be made if and when the student is either given access to, or successfully constructs, a corresponding positive instance.

For improvement to occur, students should be given appropriate exemplars, or the opportunity and incentive to rework and resubmit papers with continuous rather than single-shot access to evaluative feedback. During the reworking, students can see and participate in developing positive instances, with the tutor's help. This can help to close the feedback cycle for them. Clarifying the criteria and standards through recycling enables transfer to the next task, but does not guarantee it. Ironically, recycling in the university context usually occurs only when graduate students reach the stage of writing their dissertations.

The progressive introduction of semester courses and credit points in universities has certainly increased the range of student choice. This has been at considerable cost to other aspects of the learning environment. Short teaching blocks of twelve to fourteen weeks mean frequent transitions and a consequent lack of continuity in criterion usage. There is often no agreed set of explicit criteria. Even within a particular discipline, university teachers' expectations often differ from course to course.

Students then face the task of trying to figure out which criteria a particular teacher emphasises most. Because a teacher's appraisal often depends in part on how compatible a student's notions are with those of the teacher (whether they be ideas, opinions, or modes of expression), a student may produce a work which conforms to one particular teacher's criteria, but may be judged inferior by another teacher using a different set. In many courses, it is common for students to submit only a few pieces of work. Even if it were possible for the student to be provided with instant, comprehensive feedback, the student would still have too few cues to develop a concept of excellence in the time available.

To expect students to discover, essentially by trial and error, the relationship between a particular performance and the criteria used to appraise it is inefficient, uncertain and, in the final analysis, unjust. The more transitions there are, the more difficult it is for even very able students to improve academically, even though they may progress through a sequence of courses, accumulate credits and ultimately gain their degrees. Maybe students would be better off if we required them to attempt less, but structured the learning environment so that they achieve more.

Given the high degree of flexibility academics normally have in how they teach, and in many cases in deciding on the precise content of their courses, there appears to be considerable scope for experimentation here. If you have several colleagues who teach courses that are related to yours and who are interested in teaching more effectively, together with a cohort of students who take a number of these courses, substantial gains should be possible. Apart from the intrinsic necessity to take a more global view of teaching than is possible by a single academic working on a single course in isolation, a cooperative venture would create a supportive environment for all members of the group. Many innovations fail because the originator works alone without nourishment or encouragement. If you do proceed, document the development so that it can contribute towards your teaching portfolio, and perhaps be published later as an article.

18

Improving teaching through collaboration

Dear Jackie,

It's always great to hear of someone who puts so much of their energies into teaching, although I can understand why you feel overwhelmed by the amount of professional and personal expertise that seems to be required to do it well. Teaching is exacting and demanding work. At the same time, it can be extremely rewarding. A lot of academics derive their main satisfaction as professionals from teaching, even those who start out tentatively and lacking in confidence.

You asked for a few suggestions. Many academics, both new and experienced, say they model their approach to teaching on the university teachers they had themselves. Emulating even good teachers can, however, result in a fairly limited repertoire, especially with the introduction over the last twenty years of new approaches to teaching and assessment.

In a single letter, I won't be able to do more than outline some ideas which you can tailor to suit your own circumstances. I will start with some general comments about teaching as one of the two focal activities of a university—the other being research—then finish off with the challenges and some specifics.

Quality teaching, in an ideal world, is intended to maximise benefits for students. This implies best courses, best teaching, and best assessment. The teaching function starts with selecting from what is really a very large and constantly growing body of knowledge, then organising, structuring and packaging it to make a coherent whole. In evaluating teaching, the quality of the curriculum itself is often given only cursory attention or perhaps overlooked altogether.

In developing curriculum, not everything needs to be completely cut and dried beforehand. Some of the best teaching negotiates the content and structure of the curriculum cooperatively with the learners, and this negotiation experience is an important part of their education. In cases like these, good teaching does not happen by accident, even though unpredictable events occur. The core of the curriculum design consists of certain principles and protocols around which the course content and activities are organised.

Teaching delivery involves moving forward from the design phase, converting intentions into reality. It aims to provide students with various ways of making connections that accelerate the construction, reconstruction and extension of their knowledge. Although all learning necessarily involves some trial and error, the aim of teaching is to reduce the randomness and inefficiency of trial-and-error learning.

Some slippage between intention and reality always occurs. This can be attributed, in varying proportions, to a number of things, among them:

- ignorance of what the learners bring to the course initially,
- inappropriate assumptions about what happens in other courses students have completed or are enrolled in,

- lack of pedagogical knowledge and skill on the part of the teacher, and
- socio-cultural differences between teacher and learner.

Putting the curriculum development and the pedagogical activities together, the role of the teacher is to act as a mediator between a body of knowledge on the one hand, and student-learners on the other. In association with their colleagues, teachers are also responsible for the structure and coherence of entire degree programs, for avoiding unnecessary duplication, and for achieving complementary and mutually reinforcing outcomes across different components. As intermediaries that make it all happen, teachers occupy a position of considerable responsibility to students, employers and the community at large.

This idealisation has implications not only for the students as learners, but also for the effectiveness and efficiency of the institution as a whole. It is typically impeded, to some extent, by technically extraneous but often powerful factors such as internal politics, and the career and territorial aspirations of colleagues.

Curriculum design and delivery are two fronts on which teachers should be working. There are also two challenges. The first is the *personal development* of the university teacher, and the second is the *generation of data* on the quality of both the courses and pedagogy that will stand up to professional scrutiny. Documenting the quality of teaching in a way that can later be used in career advancement may sound to you premature and very utilitarian, but you are the only person who can make sure that appropriate records are created and maintained. There is no need to feel apologetic or self-conscious about it.

Unless university teachers are engaged in team teaching, opportunities for observing other teachers in action are normally few and far between. For this reason, I suggest you set your compass in the general direction of collaboration with other academics. This applies to teaching itself, but also to the courses and their evaluation. My rationale for promoting collaboration as a general strategy is based on a straightforward premise: those who become constructive connoisseurs of a particular process—of which teaching is only one example— develop skills that enable them to monitor and control the quality of their own activity. I deliberately use the term 'constructive connoisseur' because some connoisseurs are, quite legitimately, professional critics whose expertise is unquestionable, but who are not themselves expected to produce. By contrast, constructive connoisseurship involves a state of heightened sensitivity that appreciates in a practical sense what is required to achieve particular outcomes under a set of constraints. It is developed through having direct practical and evaluative experience within a supportive environment that is geared towards improvement, but is also prepared to tolerate experimentation, mistakes and lapses in judgment. In brief, this is why I think collaboration with colleagues holds such great promise.

Apart from improving teaching, an important advantage of working closely with colleagues who share an interest in good teaching is that it allows for the generation of credible, systematic, concrete data on the quality of teaching. These data can play a significant role in career advancement through teaching, especially when complemented by data from other sources.

Reflective self-reports are valuable tools for self-monitoring. Regardless of their insightfulness, however, they remain self-reports. They may be highly selective, or show bias in one direction (too charitable) or the other (too severe). Student evaluations of teaching obviously provide an important source of data on teaching quality, but they cannot tell the whole story. The most common source of additional information is from colleagues who teach in the same department or school.

If the person who writes a report on teaching ability has not been involved in actually teaching in a team with the person concerned, this type of so-called peer evaluation is typically unreliable, regardless of whether the comments are bland or glowing. This is primarily because the knowledge basis for the opinion is deficient. Very little of it comes from first-hand interaction or structured observation. Most of it comes from knowledge of the person outside the classroom, passing comments from colleagues and students, possibly a few contrived situations, and some chance events.

On the other hand, task-oriented collaboration and participant observation allow for critical analysis by an informed peer, especially if the evaluation side is conducted at arm's length. It also extends the vocabulary of interaction and reporting, and enables the evaluator to speak authoritatively from thorough knowledge.

The suggestions I outline below regarding teaching and courses might sound very ambitious, but don't feel daunted. The scope of the exercise can be held within whatever bounds are reasonable and comfortable for you. Having a big picture to start with, though, may help keep things in perspective while you work on a small scale initially. As success is experienced, the developmental agenda can be expanded.

TEACHING

As you yourself indicated, two possibilities for developing teaching expertise are to read up about it, or to enrol in a formal program. A lot more materials and opportunities are available now than there were even a decade ago. This is partly because of a strong international interest in the quality of university teaching, and partly because approaches to teaching are now more varied and imaginative than they ever were. Academics in general, however, report that activities such as the following are relatively ineffective in improving their teaching practice:

- listening to lectures, reading books and newsletters;
- attending conferences or workshops on teaching;
- being observed by their supervisor or a tenure committee member; or
- obtaining student feedback and ratings.

The approach that I suggest is to make good use of the excellent print and electronic materials available but then to work directly with a colleague as a critical friend. A significant part of the activity could usefully be as a participant observer in classes taught by the other teacher. If you were to audit a full course as if you were a regular enrolled student, you would attend all tutorials, seminars, workshops, problem-based sessions or laboratory classes. This type of involvement would ground your developing knowledge about teaching firmly in reality, particularly if you can establish full trust and reciprocity for the arrangement with the other person.

If you decide to work with a colleague in a quite different discipline or department, you will probably rediscover what it is like to be a complete novice in an area, struggling to learn. In the process, you may find yourself in close contact with other students, and so be able to pick up on the subtleties of how they are experiencing the teaching. As you progress through the course, you should aim to build up a composite picture of the other teacher's personal engagement with teaching, specifically their:

- enthusiasm for the subject;
- mastery of, and confidence in, the subject matter;
- desire to share it with students, and keenness to learn from students;
- provision of constructive and timely feedback to students;
- respect for students as people and as learners; and

* standards of ethical conduct with respect to teaching.

Setting up a close working relationship with someone you don't know in advance takes time and, for most people, some courage, but it can be well worth the effort. An initial invitation could be sent out on an e-mail list. You can be confident that only interested academics will reply, and you can take it from there. People are often quite willing to open themselves up if they are seriously interested in improving teaching through peer feedback.

Instead of, or as a complement to, participant observation, you might explore some possibilities with mass lectures, where it is relatively easy to be inconspicuous. You may be able to find a major lecture hall that is heavily booked for, say, three or four consecutive hours in a block each week for several weeks. Find out what classes are scheduled, and who the lecturers will be. Contact them, preferably in person, explain what your interests are, and work out what you can offer them in return. They may be interested in attending some of your lectures for a similar purpose. If you sit in on some major lectures in the early part of term, other students will be less likely to wonder what you're doing there, and you will be able to get more of a feel for what the subject is about. You may also be able to provide early reactions and feedback that the lecturer can use.

The first few observation periods should be simply ones where you look critically at the mass lecture as a total experience. Try to form a holistic judgment about its effectiveness and what seems to account for differences in quality between lecturers, and for the same lecturer from week to week. This sort of global observation is likely to provide valuable insights into the art of lecturing. To supplement this, it is often instructive to have specific 'frames' through which to view the teaching activities—if not for the full lecture, then for a significant part of it. Attached to this letter are suggestions for five such frames. This list is not exhaustive, and you may need to adapt the frames to your own circumstances. Using observational frames not only enables observers to see more overall, but also increase their personal repertoire of things to do for effective presentations to large groups. These particular observational frames will clearly be less useful for analysing and evaluating teaching in small groups because of the amount of interaction that normally occurs within sessions.

COURSES

Evaluating the quality of a course requires an analysis of what it contains and how it has been organised. Some of this can be assessed through student questionnaires, particularly the clarity of course objectives, the maintenance of direction, how satisfactorily expectations about performance are communicated, and how demanding and achievable these expectations are. Other aspects are normally beyond the students' knowledge. What is the value of excellent pedagogy if what is being taught is substandard and the students don't know it?

To make progress on this front requires a colleague who is also attuned to the requirements of good course design. The person needs to be doubly skilled, certainly an expert in the subject matter itself and also, if possible, in pedagogy of the material. The most appropriate person may well be a colleague working in the same field in another institution. Their main source of data for analysis would consist of course descriptions, statement of aims and objectives, study guides, teaching handouts, teaching support and presentation materials (regardless of media), assessment requirements, actual assessment items or tasks including tests and examinations, statements of criteria and standards, student scripts and responses to tasks.

The expert's brief would be to play the role of critical friend, seeking answers to a variety of questions such as these:

- Is the subject matter selected worthwhile, challenging, up to date, and of high priority in the field?
- Are the scope and depth appropriate to the level of the course and its context?
- Is any ideological positioning handled with integrity and professionalism?
- How adequately are the teaching strategies adapted to the subject matter, type of course, student interests and background, and the learning environment?
- How coherent is the course with respect to aims, teaching methods, student experiences, assessment processes, and learning outcomes?
- How valid and appropriate are the assessment procedures?
- Do students demonstrate high levels of achievement?
- If the course is part of the preparation for a specific profession, how well does it serve that purpose?
- How does this course compare with several others with essentially the same purpose nationally and internationally?
- Overall, what aspects need to be improved?

OBSERVATIONAL FRAMES FOR LARGE-GROUP TEACHING

Frame 1—The content of the session

Is the teacher interested primarily in disseminating information to students? Is it mostly factual material that would be more effectively obtained by other means? Does the lecture tend to be encyclopedic, with a mass of detail, or does it hit the highlights and provide a basic framework for students to use later during private study? Is the session geared towards teaching for understanding? Does it focus specifically on the problematic points that students traditionally have most difficulty in understanding?

Frame 2—The pedagogical tools used by the teacher

This frame has to do with the successful transformation of the concepts of the discipline into terms and models that are easily understood by students. What exactly does the lecturer *do* as a teacher? What is the nature of the explanatory and linking tools? How extensive is the repertoire of alternative pedagogical techniques that allow students to come at the same issue from different directions? How are these integrated, cross-referenced, and matched to the nature of the subject matter? How appropriate is the pace of presentation?

Frame 3—The media support for the session

Overhead projectors using transparencies are in common use, and increasingly teachers are using presentation graphics, video clips, and other media. Think about the quality of the media as both media and as a pedagogical tool. Is it all necessary? Is it under-used? Are the transitions from one form to another made smoothly and effectively?

Frame 4—Physical conditions and the attention of the students

Situate yourself strategically in the lecture room. Get a feel for the room itself: seat comfort, writing space, lighting level, distracting features, the temperature, background noise and acoustics. How adequate are these conditions? Instead of watching the teacher, watch the students. What is going on when they are engrossed? What seems to lead to inattention and murmuring? What brings their attention back? Do the students talk about the lecture content or presentation? How do they express frustration among themselves? Do they ask questions?

Frame 5—The teacher as presenter

How does the university teacher project into the mass-lecture role? Charisma, sincerity, personality and theatrics may all be part of it, although none of these is absolutely essential or a satisfactory substitute for more substantive aspects. How do lecturers convey enthusiasm for the subject, a desire to communicate, commanding knowledge and thorough preparation? How do they modulate their voices, maintain eye contact with students, establish their presence and control the crowd? What do they do to cope with events that are completely unexpected? Do their mannerisms interfere with the presentation?

19

Evaluating quality in teaching

Dear Shosani,

You are quite correct in saying that universities mostly pay only lip service to excellence in teaching. The gap between institutional rhetoric and actual practice is enormous. A few institutions are notable exceptions, and fortunately the number is growing. Most universities have not yet worked out clear methods for recognising or rewarding high quality teaching. Consequently they also have poor records of promoting primarily on the basis of good teaching.

A lot of research evidence shows that academics in general want an environment and the resources to enable them to teach better, and want to have good teaching rewarded by their institutions. They are favourably disposed towards learning themselves, and enjoy seeing their students learn. Faculty members say they would put more effort into developing high-quality teaching if they felt it significantly raised their prospects in the promotional stakes. I have lost count of the number of colleagues who have said: 'I put everything I have into my teaching. I find it immensely satisfying. My students do well and tell me I am a good teacher. But what's the use?' Whenever universities value research more highly than teaching, university teachers will constantly feel bullied into putting their energies into research at the expense of teaching and their students.

Although the evaluation of teaching has a vast literature and a history of at least fifty years, the real question still seems to be how universities can obtain valid and reliable evidence about teaching quality. This evidence has to withstand conceptual and academic scrutiny, be genuinely related to the teaching function, and be reasonably difficult to manipulate for the wrong reasons. In other words, the evidence needs to be substantial and specific. Furthermore, in terms of decisions about academic careers (appointment, tenure, promotion), teaching evaluation often takes place in a context that includes research evaluation as well. Because of the relative difficulty of constructing good measures of teaching, it often comes off second best.

The evaluation of research productivity is well established, despite a number of significant limitations. Research can be evaluated historically. Part of what is reviewed is the physical record of a series of publications (articles, monographs, books and book chapters), usually published over a number of years. The quality of the published research can be assessed using a variety of indicators, including impact and international standing of the journals, citations and, for books, reviews in academic or professional journals. Research grants are assessed according to whether they were secured through competitive bidding, with full refereeing processes. Competitive grants are rated more highly than commissioned or non-competitive grants, because the refereeing provides a degree of arm's-length quality control on the significance of the proposed study as assessed by academic peers. All in all, research evaluation may seem to have it made.

By comparison, university teaching does not usually involve external peer review at all. On the other hand, peer review can be organised. Properly carried out, it does produce high-quality data. As for other documentation, no records of the actual achievements of students are archived. Their term papers are usually returned to them, and their examination papers are discarded after a short while. Publications about excellence in teaching do not necessarily correspond with excellence in practice. As measures of student learning, distributions of grades awarded are highly malleable, and are mostly irrelevant to the evaluation of teaching. In addition, there is no accepted practice of cumulation as there is for research. Yet cumulation within a teaching record is just as relevant. One or two years of brilliant teaching should not carry the day. Excellence in teaching should be sustained if the institution is expected to reward it.

Formal teaching qualifications could provide part of the solution, but only if the diploma is awarded when a satisfactorily high level of teaching proficiency is attained.

Many varieties of excellent teaching occur, so no standard pattern exists. Similarly, teaching may be abysmal for a variety of reasons. Any evaluation of teaching is complex, and requires several sources of information and careful analysis. Alternative forms of documentation of teaching performance, such as the teaching portfolio, are emerging as attractive and legitimate sources of valid information on teaching quality.

The central issue is to capture a vision of teaching, what it is primarily about, and what its core elements are. The classic observation that teachers should be facilitators of learning rather than great presenters is to me the key point. So as university teachers we need to:

- develop a concept of how good teaching may be recognised, wherever and however it occurs;
- identify effective pedagogical strategies that suit the types

of interactions we have with students (one-to-many, one-to-few, one-to-one) and our own personalities and dispositions; and

- look for and detect high-quality learning in students that reflects a progressive transition from dependence to autonomy in learning.

The second of these three points involves analysing the content of the material to be mastered by the students. To what extent is it mostly factual material that would be better obtained from readily available alternative sources? How much of an intellectual framework do the students need in order to engage with it in their private study? What is the nature of the understandings students are expected to develop? What are reasonable assumptions about what students know? How can the teacher deal specifically with the most problematic points, that is, those areas that students traditionally have most difficulty understanding?

It also involves instructional design. What are the pedagogical tools available to the teacher? How can the teacher explain things? How are cause and effect to be analysed? What is the most appropriate form of authorisation the teacher can provide for statements that are made? What metaphors, models and analogic thinking suit the pedagogical task? How should the teacher provide contextualisation and other meaning-making activities? How much of the material can be taken as cut and dried, fixed knowledge? How can the teacher problematise certain issues and work with students towards solutions? What sorts of illustrations can be devised? How will they connect with the students' experiences? What use can be made of anecdote, concrete examples, illustrations and aids to memory? How are generalisations to be handled? To what extent are induction and deduction pertinent as pedagogical tools? Is it preferable to nest concepts within one another systematically, or to work towards a progressive development to a climax, or even to an anticlimax? How can students be helped to relate previous material with the present, or facilitate their memorisation through chunking? How is it best to structure repetition and recapitulation for the purpose of keeping students in the picture as to where the development is going? How does the teacher find multiple, semantically equivalent, ways of expressing essentially the same idea? To what extent will the teacher draw and work with ideas from the learners themselves?

There is plenty here for us to think about. After the purposes and pedagogy are sorted out, it is time to think about teaching and learning modes. Too often we put the cart before the horse.

What I am leading to is this: the evaluation of teaching involves a lot more than judging the surface features of a presentation to students, or simply polling the students for their reactions. Student evaluation of teaching is an important indicator, but students are in some senses uncalibrated instruments. Comprehensive evaluation of teaching involves getting to the heart of how and what students learn, and organising the circumstances and resources so that effective learning takes place. This is demanding work, obviously, but also very rewarding for us as professionals. The key issues in evaluating teaching performance are, therefore:

- the validity of performance indicators;
- the generation of relevant evidence;
- the verification of the robustness of the data, that is, its resistance to manipulation; and
- the specification of standards or degrees of excellence.

A significant factor in improving university teaching is to change the environment in which teaching takes place, and for institutions to take primary responsibility for promoting excellence in teaching. For good teaching to be recognised and rewarded, members of the committees making decisions or recommendations about appointment, progression, confirmation, promotion or prizes need to be appropriately trained and to develop a sound experiential base. Standards useful for differentiating between various levels of performance (relevant, for example, to promotion from one academic rank to the next) are only weakly determined as yet. This means that promotion committees are still in the process of constructing a body of comparative and contextualised information to provide a framework and a set of precedents for deciding future cases.

Every application for tenure or promotion that expects teaching to be taken seriously must in itself aim to be educative. The 'learners' in this instance are the committee members themselves. Every poorly conceptualised case is a lost opportunity.

I had better stop there. Looking back now over what I have written, I think I have just given you a mini-lecture on one of my favourite topics!

20

Developing cultural sensitivity

Dear Wing-Su,

Having applied for and been appointed to an academic position in this country, don't be surprised if it takes you some time to get used to the climate and the university environment. I was interested to hear your opinions of our students, even if they sometimes may behave in ways that seem to you rude and quite inappropriate.

Generally speaking, when universities advertise positions on the international market, they welcome international applicants. There is always, however, the possibility of significant cultural differences that can lead to considerable misunderstanding between university teachers and their students. These can manifest themselves in all sorts of ways. Even seemingly trivial behaviours may escalate into major issues unless the various parties come to understand one another.

Let me give you a few examples, some from my personal experience and the rest from colleagues. In each case, the issue was not a distinction between right and wrong, but of behaviour that was perfectly 'normal' in one culture but quite out of place in another.

It is not surprising when parties from two cultures meet and interact, as they have to in university teaching, that one or both parties can feel very uncomfortable with the situation, at least initially. In some of the examples below, the students came from the same cultural background as I do and the teacher came from a different one. In the other examples, the reverse applied.

Case 1

In Culture A, teachers and their students commonly address one another using their first (given) names, without any form of title. The teacher came from Culture B, where such forms of address would be taken as discourteous, and indicate undue familiarity and a complete lack of respect for the teacher as teacher. Feeling threatened, the teacher assumed that the students were not going to take their studies seriously.

Case 2

In Culture A, little account is taken of gender in appointing academic teachers, and students enrol in a course according to what the course offers for their degree programs. Students are (almost) as likely to be taught by a female as by a male. In Culture B, it is regarded as quite unacceptable for male students to be taught by a female. A cohort of male foreign students from Culture B enrolled in a particular course, which was compulsory in their degree structure. At the first class meeting, they discovered that the teacher for this course was female. They felt disturbed and refused to talk, but nevertheless tried to struggle through. In the process, they gave the teacher a hard time. Eventually it all boiled over and the underlying problem emerged.

Case 3

A university teacher appointed from Culture B was extremely well qualified and tackled teaching with enormous energy. In planning for the first part of a graduate diploma course, the teacher made a number of assumptions about the level of students' prior knowledge. In Culture B, students would have studied a certain body of material in the upper years of secondary school, and then built on this systematically during their undergraduate degrees. The students in the graduate diploma program were all from Culture A. They had not actually studied any of the 'foundation' material at school, and had been exposed to very little of it in their undergraduate programs unless they had taken specific elective courses. The teacher accused the students, who were mostly mature practising professionals, of being dumb, lazy and unfit for graduate study. Considerable tension resulted. When the teacher's assumptions were finally identified, the first reaction was total disbelief. In circumstances like these, cross-cultural university teachers need to know what is covered in the school curriculum in the state or country in which they are teaching.

Case 4

In Culture B, the teacher is regarded as the knower and dispenser of knowledge, and the student is the learner. This is looked upon as constitutive of the pedagogical relationship. The students, throughout their schooling, are used to being—indeed are trained to be—uncritically accepting of the teacher's knowledge. In Culture A, on the other hand, the 'teacher' does not necessarily know everything but is expected to stimulate sustained interactions with the students to facilitate learning. Teaching-learning theories in Culture A employ a whole vocabulary that reflects the fundamental value of mutual exchanges between teacher and learner. A teacher from Culture A taught a cohort of students from Culture B, and

found the students frustratingly passive and apparently unin-
terested. The students simply refused to engage in discussion,
to venture a personal opinion, or to provide any form of
scholarly perspective. This occurred despite the presence of
other students from Culture A who did so. The problem was
resolved when some of the assumptions about authority structures between the teacher and the learners were identified.
The Culture B students, as foreign students, had been careful
to avoid doing anything that could possibly be interpreted as
impertinence. It was also discovered that the Culture B students were abstaining from any action that could lead to
exposure in front of their fellow Culture B students, and
hence a loss of face. This would have been for them a seriously
negative and irretrievable personal event. You can also imagine
how these students reacted to the requirement that active
participation in tutorials would contribute significantly
towards a grade in the course.

Case 5

Students from Culture B were not uncomfortable about
responding in class, but a socially constructed hierarchy or
seniority ranking actually existed among the student group.
This hierarchy reflected the students' social standings back in
the country of origin, and was completely invisible to the
teacher, who was from Culture A. The teacher would regularly
ask a question of the student group generally, and then
nominate a particular student at random for a response. For
the students from Culture B, the teacher should strictly have
asked the most senior student in their group for an answer
first. If an answer was not forthcoming from that source, the
teacher could then work down through the seniority list, in
order. This would have been the correct way to do things.
The teacher had no inkling of the cultural basis for the
students' seemingly strange response patterns, and for a long

time the students did not know how to broach the subject with the teacher.

Case 6

For students from Culture B, cultural taboos required that deceased human bodies were not to be viewed except under strictly controlled social conditions, and mixed-gender discussion of certain parts of the human body was not permissible. The teacher from Culture A was unaware of this. Students from Culture B resoundingly failed their anatomy courses, partly because they had withdrawn from all laboratory sessions involving cadavers. These same students nevertheless needed a thorough knowledge of human anatomy to become professionally qualified.

Case 7

A student from Culture B was brought up in the tradition of never answering direct questions in a direct way. The correct way to reply was to start with a very broad response and then narrow it down progressively, with increasing specificity, until arriving at the core of the original question. Not knowing what was going on, the teacher from Culture A often became impatient during the converging process, and cut the response short. The student felt frustrated and insulted. It seemed to happen every time. The problem arose not because of the student's inability to frame a cogent response, but because cultural traditions demanded a spiral route to the final answer.

This list of cultural differences is meant to be illustrative, not exhaustive. Students from a particular culture often respond in ways that to them are perfectly normal, but appear quite abnormal and puzzling to a teacher from a different culture. Being insensitive is so easy.

Depending on the circumstances and your own confidence, you might find a way to raise explicitly some of these issues with your own students. Exploring the reasons for cultural differences and expectations on both sides would itself be a valuable contribution to their education.

21

Gaining entry to graduate supervision

Dear Rob,

I'm very pleased that you have been allocated some teaching in masters courses. Typically, you will find teaching at that level quite a different experience from working with undergraduates, the classes being smaller and the students generally more mature. Their professional motivation as a group will complement the freshness and youth of your first-year students, many of whom are excited about the novelty and freedom of being a university student.

I can understand why you are so disappointed at your department head's refusal to let you supervise a graduate student's research and thesis. This happens to many non-tenurable faculty members and to virtually all part-time academics, so I'm not altogether surprised. It is no reflection on you as an academic, I'm sure.

As you are probably aware, the vast majority of students in your field enrol for their graduate study as part-time students, often when their professional lives are established and they have settled down a bit. They may then be looking to advance their careers, or are simply ready to take up a new challenge. Typically, part-time enrolment involves two to four years for research masters degrees, and five to seven years for the PhD. A few students seem to go on forever.

You mentioned that your adjunct appointment is for one year in the first instance, with the possibility of a two-year extension. No doubt you are correct in saying that there is no policy within your university to preclude your being a supervisor of graduates. On the other hand, it might be useful to understand what the situation may look like from the position of the university management.

Any graduate student's research proposal will have been the result of negotiations between the department, the student and the supervisor. Suppose the university were to enrol a research student with you as principal supervisor, and at the end of the year your contract was not renewed. This could be for reasons entirely beyond your control, such as a substantial reduction in government funding or a shift in priorities within the university as a whole. This hypothetical student then could be left without a suitable supervisor. Substitute supervisors sometimes work well, but often not, depending on the circumstances. If I were your head of department, I would probably feel cautious about approving an arrangement that could possibly leave a graduate student stranded. The student would also have grounds for a formal complaint.

On the other hand, unless you get at least some exposure to, and in time carry almost full responsibility for, some research student supervision, you will not be able to develop skills or establish a profile in this area. Your own research program will be harder to get going, and your academic career aspirations will be adversely affected. Taken to its logical limit, a strict policy of not allowing a principal supervision role for contract and part-time academics prevents them from ever having the full experience of university life. I have been a member of selection committees in which a decidedly negative view was taken of applicants who had not successfully supervised a number of research students to completion. This shows a certain lack of appreciation of the career histories of, and constraints on, adjunct faculty members.

The problem is exacerbated by the current trends in universities towards casualisation, that is, using part-time or 'sessional' faculty members to do most of the teaching. Whatever full-time academic positions do come up are typically filled by people on contracts for one, two or three years.

Casualisation is a phenomenon in its own right. How well it functions in the short term depends on the availability of appropriately qualified casual teachers, particularly if the teaching is to be carried out during the daytime and there are relatively few post-doctoral students who can act as teaching assistants. It is certainly a way of making the available funds go further, but at a considerable academic cost. Casual faculty members should obviously be available for consultation with students outside class hours. Typically, opportunities for this are restricted, and the teachers are paid only for their scheduled teaching.

Casualisation usually results in a substantial drop in the ability of a school to raise or maintain its research profile, and casual faculty members are unavailable to contribute systematically to school and university administration and committee work. Finally, casualisation should automatically carry with it a number of obligatory overheads: in particular, a high-quality induction into university teaching for the large number of part-time teachers, together with appropriate supervision during the teaching. These obligations are rarely honoured.

Universities are motivated to have contract appointments because it gives them greater flexibility. New people can be hired at will, and positions can be allowed to lapse at the end of the contract term without raising issues of retrenchment, redundancy, and dismissal on the basis of unsatisfactory performance. These latter are matters that industrial unions are quite rightly very concerned about, but unions are equally concerned about exploitation of casual faculty members, and the insecurity that derives from having a series of short-term contracts rather than a long-term or permanent position.

For the most part, universities have not yet properly worked through the potential disadvantages of tenure and balanced these against the advantages that accrue from long-term continuity of employment. In addition, the supply–demand equation has shifted in recent years. University appointment committees usually find themselves being able to select from a group of very highly qualified applicants, rather than having to actively recruit new faculty members. For as long as this situation remains, many of the negative and exploitative side effects of current employment practices will persist. The whole issue is insufficiently researched and appreciated, although data are obviously available.

I will now return to your main concern, a more positive note to finish on, and a few suggestions. Obviously, conditions have to be appropriate for graduate supervision to become a possibility for short-term faculty members.

I know that the Honours students in your department complete a separate Honours year after they finish their basic degree. It is also possible under the degree rules for a full-time student to complete a research masters degree in a little over one year. If you could become involved in the Honours program, you could complement your coursework teaching with some research supervision, especially if it connects with your own research activity.

You could almost certainly help this process along by two simple strategies. First, look out for promising students who are in their second or third year of undergraduate studies, and who show high achievement and a substantial interest in the courses you teach. Raise with them the possibility of continuing into the Honours year after graduation, or even doing graduate work later. There is considerable evidence that good students are influenced by such suggestions. It gives them time to think in an unpressured way about the possibilities of advanced study, and to plan for it.

Second, develop a set of interesting research topics in your area, preferably connected with a larger theme. Make sure the size of each problem is appropriate to a good Honours project. Publicise your list within the department. Many Honours students are often at a loss to know how to identify a suitable research problem, and have only twelve months or less to carry out their investigations and write up the results. They may be open to suggestions, especially if these are accompanied by a short reading list. They can then evaluate the topics you would be willing to supervise.

Another approach altogether is to become involved in joint supervision of masters and doctoral candidates with a more experienced supervisor, and to negotiate the extent and nature of your own supervisory responsibility.

You do appear to have a major obstacle in your path at the moment. The policy itself is probably immovable, so there may be no way of literally getting *over* it. I am suggesting instead that you find ways to go *around* it by feeding into your larger 'graduate supervision' objective a range of alternative activities that are nevertheless within the same genre. These could provide experience in the supervision process that might otherwise be unavailable to you.

This is not a completely satisfactory response to your letter, but I hope it will be productive and do something to ease your frustration.

22

Climbing out of a teaching rut

Dear Lyn,

It is always good to hear from you, but not so good to find that you feel you are in a deep rut with your teaching. I don't think any of us wants to be teaching *exactly* the same course to *exactly* the same types of students for the next ten years. I sometimes wonder, though, whether my own approach and content have advanced much during the last decade, or if the same year has really been repeated ten times. *Rut* isn't a very inspiring word, is it? My thesaurus comes up with: ditch, gutter, trough, crater, trench and depression!

It might help to first look for possible causes, and a broader analysis of the situation.

- Has the rut been getting progressively deeper because you really have been doing virtually the same teaching, year in and year out? Why do you feel locked in? Who is responsible for this?
- Are you bored with the field? Do you think that the field itself is moribund and not going anywhere? Some do get that way.

- Is there a feeling of malaise that is spreading from your colleagues to you? Or from you to them?
- Which of the variables in your teaching situation do you have the power to change? Which are fixed constraints?

The first possibility is the one you hint at yourself: seek an appointment somewhere else altogether. That way you could work with new colleagues in a new institution with a slightly different ethos. Each institution does have its own ethos, regardless of how similar they all look from the outside. Besides, none of them ever has its whole act together. A change like this might be just what you need, and give you a new lease of life. If you were to take this option, transformation would obviously come about through a complete change in external circumstances.

In changing institutions you would essentially be handing over the complete responsibility to factors outside your control, except that you would choose which positions to apply for. That might be a relief, or at least a reasonable way to go. You won't know for sure until you try. One thing going for it is that it has worked for plenty of other people before you. Interest and enthusiasm have been recovered, and the adrenalin has flowed again. On the other hand, taking an entirely new appointment has to be recognised for what it is. The situation would probably be irreversible, at least in the short term.

Another possibility, this one with fewer permanent personal and family consequences, is to seek out an exchange teaching appointment with another university, perhaps in another country (for a good cultural challenge!), another city, or even in that 'other university' (as you call it) on the coast near you. Even a more or less exact exchange with a counterpart could be well worth looking at. Your graduate research supervisions could probably be arranged to follow you, with special arrangements to minimise disruptions. An exchange could provide a new slant on the courses you usually teach, temporary relief from the politics and administration of your home base, new people to meet, time to reflect and see things from an entirely new perspective, and new pedagogical challenges. Colleagues of mine who have arranged an exchange for a single semester (in one case involving house, car and pets) found that it did them a power of good intellectually and motivated them to branch out when they returned home. So an exchange is definitely worth thinking about.

A couple of agencies exist to facilitate exchanges, but you might just as easily send out an exploratory letter to, say, twenty possibilities to see if any response eventuates. Whatever the mechanism, you will need time to negotiate, whether you work directly or through an agency. Also make an early check with your personnel department and head of department to see whether your university has specific requirements or limitations that have to be attended to. For example, both universities would have to be satisfied that the exchange academic is appropriately qualified.

A third possibility is to reform your teaching through a systematic program of rejuvenation. You might not find it sensible to turn a whole course on its head in the space of one year or one semester, but you might consider turning over one third of the material, the teaching style or the approach each year for three years, testing it constantly against current needs in the field. What do other universities teach in this area? How do they organise things? You could browse on the Internet to interrogate the catalogues of other universities for descriptions of courses similar to the ones you teach. Compare them with your own, and then follow up through personal contact.

Many academics, as you know, develop and maintain a network of colleagues in other universities and research centres. Mostly these revolve around research interests, but an academic network based specifically on teaching has the potential to provide comparable stimulus and benefits.

Here are a few fronts that you could work on:

Content

Are you using materials that are relatively unchanged in the last ten years? Where has the field been going in the past few years? What is in the recent literature? What insights are offered by some of the literature *outside* the mainstream of your field? What relevance could these have for your teaching? I have often been surprised at how something that initially seems irrelevant throws some light on an issue. I scan the new journal issues in the library from an entirely different discipline just for something interesting and different to think about. Simple unfocused curiosity often turns up something that connects with my teaching or research, making me think laterally and critically.

Order of presentation

Is the current order based on a clearly discernible principle? For example, does the sequencing follow a strictly logical development (definitions, first principles, basic factual material, elaboration, policy, practice)? For the purpose of illustration, suppose that it does. The most logical order does not necessarily make the best pedagogical order. A variety of pedagogical orders can be developed, some better than others. Conceivably, the material could be sequenced historically. In many fields, that was the traditional order and sometimes still is. Another possibility would be to start with practical experience, with what actually happens in the field, then to reflect on experience, and work by induction to arrive at the core principles, along the way developing a consistent vocabulary. Alternatively, you could try building an appropriate instructional design using various pedagogical and research tools such as hypothetico-deduction, extended analogies, metaphors, positive and negative instances, and so on. Another source of ideas might be the techniques used by novelists. Explore their narrative strategies, which are often non-chronological and involve flashback, problem development and resolution, and parallel themes.

Teaching style

I know you are committed to delivering good lectures and running first-class tutorials. Maybe you should experiment with shifting some of your teaching to a resource basis to replace formal class contact for several weeks each semester. Alternatively, have you considered the possibilities of problem-based teaching?

Assessment approaches

What assessment techniques do you currently use? How satisfactory are they? Do they get to the real learning you want to assess? An interesting exercise is to interview about six students from one of your classes, two from the high achievers, two from the middle and two from near the bottom. Use the interviews to probe just what their understandings are on some of the topics you have taught. What exactly are their conceptions? Equally interesting is the question: How did they arrive at these?

Here are a few more ideas. You used to do some industrial consultancies and run professional development workshops for practitioners. Do you still do those? Can you reconnect with the professional field so you can restock your warehouse of examples, stories from real life, problems, solutions and anecdotes, and then bring them into the classroom?

Can you introduce your students to open problems, for which neither you nor the students know the answer initially? Most problems presented to students, certainly those in an examination context, are tidily structured beforehand. They are stripped of all inessential detail, simplified, and made amenable to solution. The students are given just the right amount and type of information. In such situations, the students develop and practise their problem-solving skills in an artificial and sanitised environment that is quite divorced from the world of professional work. The real world is full of problems that are diffuse, messy and hard to get a handle on. Turning unstructured or ill-structured problems into well-structured problems demands insight, imagination and sound judgment. For pedagogical purposes, the problems may not have to be structured comprehensively, just sufficiently to yield an approximate or useful solution. Can you bring your students into this process?

Relatively few university courses aim explicitly to develop these skills in their students. You could present to students the task of identifying and providing structure for the problem itself, even if the students currently have no means of solving it. This matter of problematisation and structuredness is an issue in many disciplines, not just those that lend themselves to algorithms and formal solution techniques. The humanities, liberal arts and all of the physical, social and biological sciences move ahead by identifying knowledge needs, whether these be technical and applied, practical or policy.

Finally, you have often said that most of the current textbooks in your field are effectively clones of one another. Do they have to be? What are their limitations? Could you draw together your teaching expertise, your experience as a consultant and your critical and constructive knowledge to create a text from a new perspective, or using a radically different pedagogical approach? If you think this could be a serious option for you, take advantage of some of the excellent guides now available on writing and publishing non-fiction and textbooks.

If you do decide to stay in your present position, experimentation may be an effective way to rekindle your enthusiasm and climb out of the rut.

Part four

PUBLISHING

23

Developing a
publishing program

Dear Joss,

Thank you for sending the list of your publications for me to comment on. To assess its significance from the point of view of your developing career, I will have to make a number of assumptions here and there. If I don't get these correct, you will have to make allowances.

I'll give you my overall impressions and then work from there. First, you certainly have a very extensive list of publications. Most academics of whatever rank would be envious. Second, you have published in a wide range of outlets: book chapters, professional magazines and refereed journals. Third, your publications cover an astonishing range of topics as they impinge on your profession. You seem to have been involved with a bit of everything: philosophy, pedagogy, ethics, the environment, modelling, managerialism, research methodology, and social policy. Finally, for almost all the publications in your list, your name appears as second or third author, and you have a large array of co-authors. The only two single-authored publications are book chapters.

What general signals does your list of publications send me? Drawing inferences from a publications list without having read most of the material itself carries obvious risks, but this is how it appears to me.

You have obviously been very energetic. At the same time, your collection of publications appears to lack a theme or point of convergence. The fact that you have been second or third author for nearly all of those publications seems to support this. You evidently find it congenial to work collaboratively with other researchers, and are apparently a good team player. I cannot, however, tell in what capacity you operate within these teams. Maybe you contribute to the research programs as a methodologist, data analyst, or more generally as an ideas person and critic. How did you get involved in so many different research teams? Do you find it impossible to resist becoming involved as a sidekick when asked? Are you inclined to be opportunistic?

If your research activity really is this broad, it may imply that you are not yourself moving towards the frontier of some research field. Certainly some of the people you have published with have strong reputations internationally, but in due course you may wish to strike out in a distinct direction of your own. If you do, you will also find that graduate students gradually materialise, something you mentioned you have had difficulty attracting so far.

On the other hand, there may be more conceptual commonality among your publications than I can see from the titles. You could, for instance, have a strong interdisciplinary core of research or theory that is quite appropriately expressed or applied in a variety of fields. This may explain the diversity of journals you have published in.

Truly interdisciplinary research has to create its own market until genuine interdisciplinary journals appear. When that happens, what was originally interdisciplinary starts to assume the trappings of a new sub-discipline. That is what has happened historically, and there is nothing abnormal about it. All of our current disciplines started somewhere else under different banners, and had to struggle for legitimacy and voices of their own. The boundaries could conceivably have been drawn quite differently, given a different history in the development of knowledge. You may well be doing the only thing feasible at the present time.

I commented above that the only single-author pieces in your list are book chapters. Although many book chapters are more widely read than corresponding articles, as a general rule, a book chapter 'counts' less than a good journal article for purposes of academic advancement. This is partly because of the way edited books are put together, and partly because chapters are essentially a different genre of writing from articles. Differences do exist, however, between disciplines. Book chapters are much more common in the humanities and social sciences than in the physical and biological sciences.

When an academic decides to put together an edited book on a certain topic, it may be intended primarily as readings for higher degree or advanced undergraduate students. In this case, the contributed chapters might set out, more or less in expository form, the position of the author on a particular topic or issue. The editor plays a key role in choosing the authors, and in this way influences the quality of the chapters. Frequently, reviewers of edited books comment after they are published that the quality of material in the various chapters is uneven, or that the book does not form a coherent whole. This occurs despite the best efforts of the editor to coordinate the contributions from the various authors.

On the other hand, articles in journals are expected to advance the field of knowledge. They are reviewed before publication by external referees who apply a high degree of rigour and independence. Reviewers' comments on article manuscripts often provide excellent advice to the author, and the articles are almost invariably improved as a result. In theory at least, articles are accepted for publication only when they satisfy the journal's standards.

Someone who peruses your publications list in the future may well ask themselves the same questions I did: What is this person's academic area, as defined by the research they publish? What do they stand for as an academic? How do the individual publications connect with each other and with some overall theme? Is there a line of progressive development?

If these inferences are drawn, as mine have been, from an analysis of your publications list as raw data, and if they are actually invalid, any case you make for academic advancement should make explicit reference to the interdisciplinarity of your work and provide concrete evidence.

But suppose the inferences drawn are correct. If you want to be able at some point in the future to provide strong answers to questions about focus, you need to develop your own personal publication program. The main requirement is a commitment to doing it, rather than some grand strategic plan that projects way into the future. Simply put, the aim would be to develop a cumulative, coherent research profile within a reasonable time scale, and so get closer to the leading edge of your field.

Your reputation as an academic scholar-researcher depends primarily on the quality and impact of your own published work, rather than on the reputation or ranking of your department or university. Pockets of excellence emerge and persist in some of the most unlikely places. In many situations, the calibre of research reflects the resources available, but the correlation is by no means perfect.

A side effect of a move towards a coherent research program could be that your intellectual affinities may then shift significantly towards researchers in the same field in other universities. Managing the ties you have with your present colleagues would then require some attention. You might decide that these are a very high priority for you personally, and too important to sacrifice. I am unable to offer comment on that.

An effective starting point might be some issue that has been nagging away in your mind for some time. It may be an unsolved problem, a puzzle, an enigma, an ethical dilemma, some discrepancy between theory and practice, or something you feel strongly indignant about. Focus on identifying the nub of the problem and putting a few descriptive words around it. The next step is the usual one of searching the literature in a focused way and beginning to research it. You obviously don't need any advice on how to do research, so I will concentrate on the 'program' idea.

While working on the primary front, run a secondary agenda that looks for related, ancillary or intriguing side issues that have the potential to mature into future research topics. Record these as they appear. Some of the readings or research findings on your primary topic will feed in to one of the secondary items, and all of this should be noted.

In my own work, I often find that a process of 'budding' seems to occur. Most of my work is analytical and conceptual. While I am in the process of writing, some lateral thoughts usually occur to me, sometimes quite suddenly. I call them 'thoughtfalls'. Mostly I don't quite know where they come from, and occasionally they arrive when I am doing something quite removed from academic life. They are typically related to my topic, but do not necessarily appear central at first.

I pursue these far enough to see whether they are, or could be made to be, relevant to my present argument. If it turns out that they do not contribute significantly enough to the theme to be incorporated into the main text, I snip them off, but I don't throw them away. I put them into another folder. In due course they may become the seeds of another piece of research. Many do; a lot don't. This is what I mean by budding.

I take care when I snip a bud. Because this related but

distinct idea occurred to me while I was writing on the main topic, my reasoning is that it may also occur to one of the referees who will read the manuscript critically for a journal. The referee may then think: Doesn't this author see that this could be extended further or that it has a related application? So where I snip off the bud, I may include a sentence that says something like: 'This is an important topic in its own right, but to pursue it would take us beyond the scope of the present paper'.

I could take you back through my list of publications and show you how most of the articles grew in some way or another out of previous ones. Although I have used budding to describe this process, I nevertheless try to ensure that all my articles have a demonstrable connection with my overall academic field. I do not want them to be, or to appear to be, like a random walk through the forest.

Let me summarise. People who read your CV in the future should be able to see some kind of consistent theme. In your case, I had difficulty finding it from the information you sent. I suggest you aim to position yourself so that, in a few years' time, you can review your work and see how the various aspects of your research career are linked together in a conceptual and developmental way. The objective should be to work on a reasonably coherent research and publishing program, not simply to grow a collection of publications.

24

Organising a publication syndicate

Dear Ansell,

I agree with you that being an academic can be a pretty lonely experience. There are, however, a number of ways to foster collegiality, and they do not depend for their success on what we normally regard as personal friendships, although close friendships may develop out of them later.

I have had considerable success working with small groups of faculty members on more or less exclusively academic activities in what I call 'publication syndicates'. These take some effort to set up and maintain but are effective in providing a constant stimulus to productive thinking and action, especially in relation to developing a publication profile. A syndicate is ideal for faculty members who feel that they lack experience in academic publishing, lack confidence in their ability to publish in high-quality journals, or lack the knowledge and skills to deal with editors and reviewers. It is all about creating a supportive, collegial and productive environment. This is how the syndicates I have been involved in work; you may need to make adjustments to suit your own circumstances.

The syndicate itself simply consists of a group of like-minded academics who agree to act cooperatively to further their mutual scholarship and publication. The members should be committed to the task of accelerating the production of either manuscripts for publication in academic journals, or chapters for publication in edited books. The idea works well for people who need encouragement and support, who want to learn the skills and approaches needed for academic publishing, and who are prepared to help one another. The term syndicate refers to how the group manages its affairs, and has no implications for whether the authorship of the publications is single, joint or multiple. It can handle them all.

The number of members is usually between four and six. To ensure continuity, all members agree to commit themselves to the syndicate for a minimum period of six months. My experience has been that unless members are prepared to commit themselves to full meeting attendance and participation, the syndicate collapses fairly quickly.

Having a common research field is useful but not necessarily a prerequisite for an effective syndicate. In fact, it often helps to have one or more fringe members in the group, because their demands for clarity and precision in expression are more acute. These members ask the simple questions that often turn out to be profound. A spin-off when there is a spread of interest areas is that everybody comes to learn a lot about, and to respect, other fields and research approaches.

Apart from some committed colleagues, the syndicate needs some raw material to get started and to continue. Normally, this consists of drafts of articles produced by syndicate members. A draft paper may be based on recent research data arising from a project, but other possibilities exist. For example, members may have written something a long time ago that never got past the first stage, a conference paper that contains important ideas but was not further developed after the conference, notes for an address delivered to a professional or lay meeting that contain original concepts or proposals, a submission made to an official inquiry that contains material about the interaction between elements of the discipline and public policy matters, innovative insights into university teaching, or some partly processed research data that so far have seemed to defy all attempts at finalisation. All of these are potential starting points. I have found that most academics have something to draw on, although in the past they may have felt some blockage in bringing it to completion.

Being a syndicate member does not necessarily oblige a member to produce a first draft of a paper within a fixed time. Some participants will be self-starters and quick off the mark. Others will join primarily for the external framework and support a syndicate provides, and will have something to offer only after they develop some confidence. A few members may work on several manuscripts at once. This may help them to maintain a sense of continuing progress if a particular paper temporarily runs aground.

The main vehicle for the syndicate to achieve its aims is the colloquium, which is simply a structured meeting to discuss a draft of a member's manuscript. The colloquium is an academic meeting, not a social event. The goal of each meeting is to move a manuscript from its initial state, whatever that may be, at least one step ahead towards publication. In our syndicates, we do not place any limits on the number of drafts a particular paper can go through on its way to finalisation. Manuscripts are designated by number rather than title, because titles may well be modified during the course of article development. Keeping the same number avoids confusion.

The frequency of colloquia is tailored to the level of

activity. A useful starting point is to agree to meet on a regular basis every third week for about an hour and a half. Compared with meeting solely on demand, I have found regular meetings to be preferable, because all members then write the times in their diaries in advance and work their other commitments around them.

The syndicate appoints a convenor, who acts as a sort of manager. Among other things, the convenor confirms the time and venue for each colloquium and reserves a place in the colloquium schedule for each draft paper as it is produced. If activity shows signs of flagging, the convenor does a little prodding and encouraging of members who are not producing. The convenor acts as overall coordinator of the publishing program and maintains a file of the latest versions of all papers currently in the system. A display folder is adequate for that. Although the convenor acts in that role for a reasonable period of time for the sake of continuity, the position of chair at colloquium meetings is rotated. Generally, the chair at a colloquium should not be the author whose paper is being discussed.

A manuscript draft is distributed by the convenor about one week before the colloquium meeting. Members read through the paper carefully, and make any comments they think are relevant in a reasonably legible form, because the author needs to be able to read them later. They bring their annotated copies to the meeting.

It is useful to distinguish between macro and micro levels of interaction. The macro level has to do with the big picture: gist, structure, logical consistency, overall tone, flow of the paper as a whole, appropriateness of the approach for the intended audience, and major issues or points of view that the author may need to take into account. The micro level has to do with detailed structure: paragraphing, headings, sentences that need to be clarified or reworded, sections (including sentences or paragraphs) that could be repositioned, grammatical points, typographical errors, and residual ambiguities. The reason for having two levels is that it is a waste of time to work on micro issues until the macro issues have been resolved. There is no point in suggesting grammatical corrections to sentences or paragraphs that will have to be discarded or completely rewritten anyway.

In the first stage of a colloquium meeting, the chair asks each member in turn to make a brief statement giving an overall impression of the paper, or a reaction to it. To ensure that each person present gets an opportunity to make at least an initial comment, discussion does not begin until the last person has made a statement. The author may, however, ask for clarification on the way round. This tactic reduces the likelihood that early comments drive the agenda, placing later contributions from members at a disadvantage. When all participants have had an opportunity to comment, open discussion proceeds. The author or any other person may seek elaboration, make suggestions or ask questions. Naturally, the author is obliged to consider all comments of other syndicate members, but is not bound to make use of them.

Discussion is not allowed to degenerate into personal criticism or attack, regardless of the state of the paper to be discussed. Some initially jumbled, confused and poorly expressed messes of ideas turn out as very fine articles in the end. To maul a paper savagely in its early drafts merely to score points over colleagues does no one any good.

After this general discussion, the convenor, in consultation with the author and the meeting as a whole, and taking into account the time available, decides whether to work through the paper page by page—discussing points of substance, logic or style, and smoothing any remaining rough edges—or to terminate the colloquium if major revisions and rewriting are obviously called for.

At the conclusion of the colloquium, the participants quickly leaf through their copies of the manuscript to scratch out any matters that have been dealt with satisfactorily, or that are then clearly irrelevant in the light of the discussion. They then give their copies to the author, who can go through the annotations for additional small points or queries at leisure. The author eventually returns the copies to the respective syndicate members.

If the embryonic syndicate group has no expert with a proven record in academic publishing, it has to explore ways of getting itself off the ground. An effective strategy is to include the study of at least one published article on the agenda for several early colloquia. Published articles are not of uniformly high quality, and it is instructive to identify what makes the difference between an outstanding article and a mediocre one.

The members analyse each article from both substantive and structural points of view. What is the content of the article? How does this content integrate with existing knowledge? What contribution does the article itself make to the body of knowledge in the field? What is the form of the abstract? What are the characteristics of the introduction and conclusion? How is the body of the article structured? How is the argument framed? What and how are any generalisations made? How is supporting evidence presented? This analysis is followed through by writing a 'reviewer's report', recommending actual publication, publication subject to specific amendments, complete reworking, or even rejection!

A second option is to make some initial headway on a manuscript by putting it through several revisions, then to obtain an honest, objective opinion by inviting a more experienced colleague with a record of successful publishing to attend one or two colloquia as a guest.

Working closely together in a syndicate setting often leads to changed, and sometimes quite original, ideas and perspectives generated not by the author but by other members. Our policy has been that all ideas and comments that arise during discussion automatically become the property of the manuscript author at the end of each session. This includes a new term, a telling insight, a particularly apt phrase, or a well-expressed sentence. The justification for this is that contributions are always generated within the context of a forum, so single ownership of an idea is arguable anyway. Besides, trying to keep track of all the bits would quickly become unmanageable. This sort of generosity actually promotes a lot of goodwill. Now and then, one of the participants may actually give away an idea that turns out to be seminal. We all accept that.

We often make a tape recording of the colloquium discussions. Worthwhile ideas that could strengthen and improve a manuscript often arise on the run. Although many of these points will be noted down by the author as a matter of course, sometimes they seem to just vanish when the author tries to recapture the thought or the exact wording. Having a recording is easy insurance against this.

The syndicate also plays an important role in helping an author handle a rejection. The reviewers' comments and the letter from the editor are read and discussed at a regular colloquium, but preferably not immediately after receipt, along with the author's response. Because producing the manuscript has involved the whole syndicate, it makes sense for the syndicate to also help the author retrieve the situation.

Naturally, you will have to develop and refine a set of procedures for your own circumstances, but I have found the publication syndicate idea to be productive and immensely satisfying. I hope you can do something with it yourself.

25

Weighing conference papers against journal articles

Dear John,

Thank you for sending me a copy of your CV, which was assessed by your tenure committee. Judging from the feedback report, the committee obviously noted the large number of conference papers you have delivered, but was concerned about the small number of refereed journal articles you have published. You consider this unfair and narrow-minded.

In my view, the committee has a case, as I will explain. Obviously I will not be referring to your conference papers in particular, because I have only read one or two of them, and heard you present at one conference. The issue is about conference papers in general.

In the first instance, papers for conferences are very often accepted on the basis of a short abstract of perhaps 150 words. This abstract provides the basis for a judgment about the quality of the forthcoming paper. In practice, what usually happens is that the bulk of the paper proposals are accepted.

The conference participants then are expected to prepare their papers to meet the specifications in the abstract.

Some conference organisers state that all proposals for papers, posters, or symposia are *refereed*. This suggests that there is some kind of quality control on the papers to be delivered. In my experience, the rigour of the refereeing procedures is often not particularly high. Once a proposal is accepted, the paper is through the conference gate. The paper itself, when it is delivered, is not subject to further quality control.

Two consequences follow from this fairly liberal policy of paper acceptance. The first is that the conference is larger than it otherwise would be, and this brings kudos to the sponsoring organisation and the organisers personally. In some cases, several sessions have to be run simultaneously, often with different themes. The second consequence is that many of the attendees are able to obtain assistance towards conference registration fees, fares and accommodation on the grounds that they are to present a paper that has been refereed. Naturally, institutions differ as to the levels and ways they support conference attendance, but this arrangement is not uncommon.

I now come to the content of the conference papers themselves. These are often prepared with a view to oral presentation within a fairly limited delivery time. Conferences I go to may have several speakers in a session. Speakers are allotted, say, twenty minutes for delivery followed by, if they're lucky, five minutes for questions. The oral presentation consists of a stream of words delivered at more words per minute than anyone can read printed text, often moderated by body language and even humour during the presentation. The audience can rarely pause and reflect deeply on what is being presented, except at the risk of missing what the speaker is about to say. Critical academic debate, if it occurs at all, is often truncated by the need for the chair to keep the session rolling and on time, to be fair to all speakers.

The energy put into preparing conference papers varies greatly, but they are often not prepared until the week before the conference begins. More than a few academics have found themselves staring at the abstract they wrote previously, wondering how they can possibly deliver on it! It was written in a flash of optimism when the call for papers was made months earlier. Very few good journal articles can be produced within one week.

An article published in a good journal requires a much more disciplined approach. The peer review process that takes place before an article is accepted for publication is a careful, formal affair. In most cases, the original manuscript is read by two reviewers who are experts in the field. If they provide specific feedback, the author may be required to do further work on the paper before it is finally approved for publication. If the manuscript does not reach a publishable standard, it is rejected outright and may never see the light of day. Poor quality articles reflect badly on the journal, the editors and the reviewers.

Articles are not transient events. After publication, they are absorbed slowly by the reader, can be checked and rechecked for internal consistency or logic, and compared at leisure with other research reported in the literature. Articles are obviously open to much wider and deeper scholarly scrutiny than conference papers. They are routinely indexed and abstracted and thereby made accessible to researchers around the world. Conference papers, even if they are published in proceedings, often reach only a limited audience and are often inaccessible through library reference services.

When academic committees are assessing the research output of faculty members, you can be sure that most of the members of the committee are familiar with the procedures for acceptance and dissemination of both conference papers and journal articles, and know that the two are not comparable. This is the basis for the different weightings. When this principle is understood and extended to various other academic activities, it provides a useful foundation for academics to work out their priorities for time and effort.

I am not saying that presenting papers at conferences is a waste of time. In some disciplines, presenting scientific findings in a conference paper that is then published in the proceedings is *the* standard way to announce a research discovery, and is highly valued.

In any case, attending a conference can be an important way to build or consolidate one's personal academic network. It can also provide a good opportunity to present work that is in progress, to test emerging ideas, and to use questions and responses from the audience to shape further research or to help turn the conference paper into a journal article. The article is, however, a genre of its own.

26

Resolving joint authorship

Dear Anna,

In your recent letter, you said you intended to have a discussion about possible authorship arrangements with your supervisor, even though your doctoral research is only in its early stages. I realise that your PhD is being undertaken as a full three-year research program without any course work, so I will focus my remarks on that. Broadly speaking, that sort of program should give rise to a few good refereed papers.

As you know, some supervisors demand to have their names first on all articles arising out of their students' doctoral research. Some graduate students have felt quite exploited through their post-PhD publishing experience as a result. Other supervisors expect their students' names always to be first, and yet others decide each case on its merits.

Unless all parties agree that the distribution of credit is fair, tension can arise between supervisor and candidate. In the worst cases, this can lead to lifelong animosity, and stands in stark contrast to the strong collegial relationship that usually develops during candidature. The issue is too impor-tant to leave up in the air, or to leave to the supervisor's preference alone, so having a discussion about it now is definitely timely.

Although your letter was specifically about publications arising from a PhD program, some of what I am about to write applies with equal force to regular grant-assisted research programs. High-level research assistants also can become involved in the authorship issue.

Apart from the issue of scientific discovery, which I discuss below, it really does matter whose name is first in the list of authors. People who peruse CVs usually assume that the first author was the principal investigator or contributed most to the research, unless there is something on the paper itself to indicate that a different principle was used. It is also important because the first author's name is usually the key in abstraction and citation indexes. Finally, other researchers' in-text references to articles with three or more authors typ-ically mention only the first author's name, followed by *et al.* This author then gets most of the informal publicity and credit. I know of two researchers who have published joint papers for decades. They say they decide the order of authors' names for each article by a coin toss. Their field happens to be probability, but in any case both are already well established in their careers, so the stakes are not high.

You asked me about the general rule for the order of authors' names. In fact there is no universal rule. Disciplines vary in their practices, and these often reflect differences in the ways doctoral work is organised. I will describe below two contrasting situations to illustrate, making a few simplifying assumptions along the way so that the explanation does not become too complicated. Many disciplines fall somewhere between the two.

In the sciences and technologies, and excluding purely theoretical work, doctoral research is frequently undertaken in a team setting. The candidate joins a project team, and is typically allocated a relatively self-contained part of a much larger enterprise to research, under the supervision of the project director. Essentially, the doctoral student locks into the supervisor's ongoing research program for the period of candidature. A key outcome for the candidate is training in high-level theorising and research technique. This training is then usually followed by a series of post-doctoral appointments, often in other universities, to broaden and deepen research experience and expertise. The person then embarks on a more independent research career.

In this situation, most of the conceptualisation and specific hypothesising will have been done already by the leader of the research team, before the graduate student's candidature begins. Suppose that the ongoing research program has the possibility of achieving or contributing to a major scientific discovery. Most research programs at least aspire to this, even if it is not always realised. The chief investigator would be fully justified in expecting to be regarded as the 'discoverer', rather than ceding that right to a graduate student who happens to spend a relatively short period working on the project while doing a doctorate. The chief investigator's name should, therefore, legitimately come first on any formal publications. The graduate student should appreciate the potential magnitude of the stakes involved in scientific discovery, and recognise the right of the chief investigator to have authorship priority, regardless of who does most of the actual writing.

In a number of fields, however, candidates often begin doctoral studies after having established themselves in a professional career in the social, health, engineering or biological sciences, or in the visual or performing arts. If they subsequently join a university to take up academic work, these faculty members obviously bring a wealth of experience that enriches their teaching. It also means, however, that the topics they wish to research for their PhDs are likely to follow, at least in part, from interests developed as a professional in the field and which are probably consistent with their areas of teaching. This situation applies even more strongly when people who remain in their professional posts decide to do doctoral studies on a part-time basis. The tendency then is for them to negotiate topics that connect directly with their professional lives.

In these cases, the supervisor typically provides substantial help in framing the topic, particularly in relation to breadth and depth, so that the research is appropriate for a doctoral degree. This may take six to nine months, or even longer. Science candidates sometimes find it hard to understand how humanities and social science candidates can spend such a long time working out what they are supposed to be researching. Instead of clear hypotheses to be tested, there are 'issues' to be explored or a 'small-t thesis' to be developed and argued. The boundaries of the topic, the conceptualisation of the study and, perhaps to a lesser extent, the research approach are essentially of the candidate's making, although shaped or carried out under the guidance of a supervisor. The supervisor mainly provides high-level critical input into problem definition, research methodology, refinement of the argument line and polished writing.

The candidate is, effectively, the principal investigator and progressively takes on ownership of the project. Where this particular characterisation of doctoral research applies, the person who designs and researches their 'own' topic is surely entitled to have first-author billing on publications, because their intellectual investment in the dissertation is very high. The intellectual property dimension to a decision on authorship is therefore extremely important. For this reason, also, the doctoral study can play a more significant part in establishing the person in an academic field. The dissertation, if you like, stakes out some academic territory, especially when post-doctoral fellowships are not the usual path to a research career. Students who complete a doctorate primarily as a qualification do not necessarily build a research profile on the basis of work done for their dissertations, but for faculty members the PhD is often the launching pad for a continuing research program.

You mentioned a concern about possible exploitation. For me, exploitation occurs when benefits accrue to one party at the expense of another party. It is a particular danger when a large differential in power exists. Obviously, the best arrangement is to aim for an even-handed win-win situation, with the benefits being shared in a way that is commensurate not only with the scientific or social significance of the outcome and the levels of input, which is what the discussion above is mostly about, but also with long-term career benefits. Considerable advantages can flow to a candidate who is a joint author with an eminent researcher, even when the candidate's name is not first. Except in science and technology, researchers who are already first author on 200 papers probably do not enhance their reputation or career prospects further by always insisting on being first author with every graduate student. Inputs and potential career benefit need to be balanced in coming to a decision.

A final factor to consider is: who designs the journal article, gives it substance, and does the actual writing? In most cases, the scope, intended target journal, and structure of the manuscript will be a joint affair, with the candidate drafting the text after the basic decisions have been made.

You implied in your letter that your supervisor expects to have first listing for all subsequent works associated with the topic you researched. That is an appalling idea! A supervisor's claim during or immediately after candidature is one thing. A perpetual claim on your own scholarship is preposterous.

Despite the principles I have outlined above, it still may be worth checking whether your institution has a policy about joint authorship. Maybe it has some guidelines, but a strict rule is probably too much to expect. As I have indicated, the matter is certainly more complicated than simply who provides the labour. It involves, among other things, the origins of the research topic, notions of intellectual property, the nature of contribution to a manuscript and possibly the relative benefits that will accrue to both parties. All of these involve sound judgment and ethical consideration, rather than the simple application of a rule.

When you come to supervise your own research students for their higher degrees, you can see why you should discuss early in their candidature the question of authorship of articles or a book that might arise out of the research.

27

Analysing an editor's rejection

Dear Peter,

The copy of your manuscript arrived safely a week ago. I have now read it through, together with the editor's and the reviewers' comments. A rebuff like that is never pleasant. But if, as you say, you sent it to that journal because it really is the best international one in the field, you naturally can expect it to have very stringent standards. The tone of the editor's covering letter is not unfriendly, but it does not hold out a lot of hope either, at least on the surface. Like every other manuscript, yours will have had to compete with others available about the same time. The editor sees the whole array of manuscripts sent in, and tries to publish only the best material.

Because you asked me for an independent opinion about your manuscript, I decided not to read the reviewers' reports beforehand in case they biased my thinking. So I read your paper cold, then wrote out my comments. When I read the reviewers' reports afterwards, my reactions and theirs overlapped substantially in content.

The editor's decision does depend to some extent on the choice of reviewers. You said that the reviewers' comments seemed particularly savage and cutting. The comments they made are certainly critical, but there's no need to assume that the reviewers were unduly prejudiced against your type of paper or the country you come from. When I get an editor's rejection letter, which I do from time to time, I usually read the comments immediately. I then put the comments and the manuscript aside for a couple of weeks before reading them again. My theory is that if I come back to them when the bruise has started to heal, I am in a better frame of mind to see exactly what the reviewers have said. I can then decide whether and how to improve the paper. Sometimes I incorporate the material into something else, or occasionally scrap it altogether.

I know you put a huge amount of time, effort and care into the research project and into getting this paper written. How is it that the reviewers haven't been able to recognise this and recommend that the paper be accepted? The reviewers didn't actually know how much work was involved, and couldn't have taken it into account if they did. All they had was the manuscript. The reviewers' job was to say whether the manuscript was publishable as it was, could be reworked, or should be abandoned.

When you contacted me, you asked for an honest opinion. Do I think the paper is eventually publishable? Is it worth the effort of trying to revise it, and submitting it elsewhere? In brief, there are several interesting ideas in this paper, but they are lost in the verbiage. If they were distilled and then clearly explained, there might be an article in it. On the other hand, these ideas might be better incorporated into a larger paper that makes a more substantial contribution to research in the area.

Your abstract and opening paragraph certainly make strong claims about the significance of the paper, and how it advances the conceptualisation of your field. Neither the reviewers nor I were convinced that your paper delivered satisfactorily on that promise. Spending a lot of time in the introduction of a paper to convince the reader how seminal and important the findings are is usually not helpful. On the other hand, the paper has to be contextualised and say where it is going, so there has to be a balance.

In your case, toning down the front end is not the solution. The problem is not really with the promise being too ambitious, but with whether the paper represents a significant enough advance in the field to be worth publishing. Every piece of work adds something to our thinking. Every manuscript is unique, if only because it represents a new synthesis or a new way of looking at a particular issue. What the reviewers had to decide was whether the quantum of new knowledge in your paper was enough to warrant publication.

When I finish reviewing a manuscript, I ask myself: what do I know now that I didn't know when I started? I definitely want the paper to extend my knowledge base. Trying to quantify the size of an advance in research is a difficult exercise, but the issue implicitly has to be addressed every time a manuscript is reviewed. Abstract arguments could go on forever, but pragmatics demand that there is some threshold. Below that, the paper does not deserve to be published; above it, it does.

You said you were surprised that one of the reviewers was so pedantic about matters of format and style, and that the reviewer should have been able to see past those shortcomings. I only partly agree. Although many reviewers do not comment at all on occasional lapses of grammar or style, a pronounced weakness in a manuscript sends a negative message to the reviewer, and it is not really the reviewer's job to patch things up. This reviewer was obviously annoyed because the presentation did not comply with the preferred style for the journal, and so that struck a constantly jarring note. Some manuscripts have such a stream of technical lapses that a reviewer has difficulty with the flow of the paper because of the repeated interruptions. The same person did, however, make a lot of additional substantive points, and they are similar to those from the other reviewer.

You wondered whether you should try another journal because of the hostile referees. This is probably too harsh on the reviewers. If a paper is written interestingly, and if it does have something substantial to offer, it will be obvious to the reviewers, and ultimately to all readers, that publishing it was the right decision. The extent and perceptiveness of your reviewers' comments show that they have been anything but dismissive of your manuscript. They have given it a lot of care and attention, and suggested ways it could possibly be redeveloped. Some of those improvements would involve additional research, or at least using the data you already have to tackle a supplementary question.

In general, I would not be reluctant to send a revised manuscript to the same journal simply on the grounds that it might go to the same reviewers. If a manuscript does go to the same reviewers after a reasonable time interval, they would probably take it at face value the second time round and evaluate it on its merits. The first versions would long ago have been shredded or returned to the editor. Most reviewers wouldn't have the time or the interest to track down and re-read their original comments when they receive a thoroughly reworked manuscript. Life is too short to spend time figuring out whether authors have taken note of some earlier criticism on a manuscript that is no longer to hand. If you do decide to redevelop this manuscript, send it to the journal that best suits it in its revised form.

I have generally been appreciative of the perceptive comments made by anonymous reviewers. Editors often provide guidance as to how to interpret the referees' evaluations, and this advice is well worth considering. On a few occasions, reviewers have saved me from stumbling into a trap. On others, they have pointed me in very fruitful directions, or suggested points that needed to be clarified. Occasionally, they have misunderstood the point I was trying to make, which means I had not explained myself properly. A couple of times I have had reviewers who were categorically wrong about certain matters of fact, so that had to be demonstrated to both editor and reviewers. The result of the review process in my experience has always been that the manuscripts have been substantially improved.

You should not lose heart simply because the paper has been rejected in the first instance. A very substantial proportion of papers, up to 70 per cent in some disciplines, that are returned to authors with critiques by the reviewers are significantly improved and ultimately published as a result. This lifts the reputation of the journal, its editors and the authors even though it adds to the time taken for publication. On the first submission of one of my articles, the editor wrote the fatal line: 'I regret to inform you . . .' After it was thoroughly reworked for a different, equally ranked journal, the new editor wrote: 'I am very pleased to be able to tell you that we shall be publishing your paper in issue number . . . We are very glad that you chose to send it to us.'

I hope your revision goes well, and that you have a better outcome for the next version.

28

Measuring research productivity

Dear Bray,

There is a certain logic to your argument. Three articles in refereed journals are not enough for promotion, but 200 articles would certainly lead to success. Other things being equal, what is the magic number between three and 200 that is the (unofficial) threshold? I have been asked that question quite a few times by colleagues, using essentially the same reasoning. Unfortunately there is no such magic number.

The explanation lies to a large extent in the way the promotion committee assesses an applicant's research and scholarship. Many people have said to me in the past that all the promotion committees do is count the number of articles published in refereed journals to see if the faculty member is over the line.

In my experience it simply does not work that way. I have never been a member of an appointment, tenure or promotion committee that has not seriously weighed up all the factors together. Committee members always take note of the number of scholarly publications, but for the most part they also try to work through the tricky business of balancing quality versus quantity. They do this in a deliberate attempt to recognise the differences between fields and approaches to research and productivity. Here are some examples of why differences need to be taken into consideration.

First of all, I take it we are talking about an accumulated body of research publications, not an annual rate. In some fields, one or perhaps two substantial articles or creative works each year sustained over a number of years would be regarded very highly. In other fields, articles typically report specific findings, are relatively short (maybe only two or three pages long), and are produced in considerable quantity as a normal product of ongoing research projects. So what counts as a 'reasonable output' depends on the context and the norms in the discipline or academic field.

That being said, some faculty members have a reputation for their factory approach to creating journal articles. They are into assembly lines and mass production, and generate an astonishing output. All of the papers follow more or less the same structural formula. They are all well written, and the author spreads them across a large number of journals in different sub-fields, where they each appear to contribute something novel. But if an expert in the field looks closely at the whole body of work, it is seen to be what they are: little more than variations on a theme. Each article adds very little to the total store of knowledge. For this reason, many universities send a sample of an applicant's best publications, as nominated by the candidate, to outside experts in the field for an independent, rigorous assessment of their contribution to the discipline. This procedure is especially important for promotion to senior academic ranks because of the level of leadership expected. None of this is meant to discourage or devalue the popularisation or cross-seeding of a key idea in several fields. This can be very important.

Let me illustrate from the other extreme. An academic might spend two or three years writing and refining an article that breaks entirely new ground in the field, and is later cited extensively. In your own field, maybe you can identify a book (or three or four articles) published in the last twenty years, that have redirected your field in terms of key ideas, findings or method, and that are widely cited today. Most disciplines have a few such examples. Relatively rare though these are, logically they should count as outstanding contributions to the advancement of knowledge. The significance of research output, therefore, cannot be settled simply by counting publications.

Even citation counts have their problems. Promotion criteria typically place a premium on articles published in refereed journals of international repute, and also on the number of citations of those articles. Although measuring research output and impact by these means may seem to have obvious validity, citation counts (discounted for self-citations and friend-citations) miss the true story in particular situations.

Take the case of a researcher with a substantial research monograph. Suppose it attracts very little attention in the first few years after publication, and that this is because it challenges the dominant research ideology or what is taken as orthodoxy in the discipline. Some such works initially find a lot of difficulty getting published. When they are published, they may be treated as maverick contributions in terms of the accepted norms. Not many other researchers take them seriously at the time. A decade later, however, a monograph of this kind might be highly acclaimed and widely cited. It may even play a role in transforming a discipline into something substantially different. Most universities would want to retain and promote a researcher who achieves this sort of result, because it is exceptional. Sometimes a university will come to appreciate the significance of the work too late to have prevented the person from taking a senior position elsewhere.

Consider a quite different scenario, still with this hypothetical monograph in mind. The work may be well-intentioned and initially influential. Subsequent, more thorough developments, however, show it to be categorically in error in key respects, and to have led a suite of research projects up some futile path. In turn, this leads to the generation of many critical or counter responses, and consequently citations! Bad research sometimes produces copious citations, but the pure count may be spurious. If through this research, however, one avenue of investigation is fully explored and then closed, it may not be spurious at all. Knowing that the solution to a problem definitely does not lie in a particular, initially promising direction is not the same as knowing nothing. Elimination of possibilities is often an important step in making progress on the broader front.

Two more examples. When an article contains important methodological insights, it may rarely be cited in refereed research articles, but be prescribed as required reading for a host of graduate-level courses internationally, and be referenced extensively in books and book chapters. This influence is invisible through the normal citation counts. Finally, a breakthrough in investigative technique may, in some settings, quickly become standard practice and replace all of the earlier inferior methods. Once it becomes almost universal, it is not news any more and nobody needs to cite it.

An important factor in weighing up the value of research is that most of the people on the hiring, probation and promotion committees are themselves people working within the system. If they already hold high academic rank, they will have been judged in the past by their peers, in roughly similar circumstances, using similar criteria. If they are junior members of the committees, they themselves will be hoping for honest and fair treatment at the hands of their colleagues. In the process of deliberation, the committee has to make just and defensible decisions about people whose teaching and research achievements are in fact substantially different and whose careers will be significantly affected. This does not amount to a claim that committee decisions are always the right ones, or that extraneous influences are always kept out.

You mentioned, too, about not being part of a research team and not being a big grant recipient. You fear that this will reduce your long-term prospects. An obvious rationale for what is known as performance-based funding, which financially rewards either teaching excellence or research excellence, is that it provides a concrete incentive for researchers to be productive. It imposes an extrinsic value on the work being done. Blindly applied, it can lead to anomalies and injustice. For example, some researchers are able to do world-ranked research primarily by using their brains as the research instrument. The stereotypical don who writes on the backs of old envelopes still exists. At the other extreme, some faculty members break up a piece of research into ten short articles instead of publishing the longer monograph that the research deserves. Systems that ignore or penalise the first of these and reward the second should be deplored.

An obsession with the number and value of research grants obtained, or the number of articles or monographs published, will, in time, distort the whole research enterprise. The more that research productivity is codified and formularised, the more it may appear to be open and fair. At the same time, it will be progressively removed from sound, professionally accountable judgments.

This presents a small number of academics with a real dilemma. On the one hand, they may be well positioned to produce a work of considerable significance every few years, or maybe one large piece as a major contribution of an academic lifetime. Many of us will retire without publishing a seminal work, I'm afraid! At the same time, they may be seen by their colleagues as not contributing at all to departmental resources by attracting research grants, infrastructure support and research assistant salaries in the competitive stakes.

Sooner or later, somebody is going to ask whether the method of funding and recognition that currently operates is the best one in terms of contribution to knowledge, particularly for things that matter from the points of view of industry, society, sustainability and ethics. The big unknown in any study that researches those issues is trying to estimate the quantity and form of the knowledge that would have been produced had the external conditions been set up to recognise and reward it.

Anyone who differs from the mainstream is always faced with the task of explaining why they see things differently and value their work differently. For my money, a substantial work that represents a real advance in knowledge is worth far more than a plethora of essentially trivial results, regardless of the time, resources or method used for generating any of them. For purposes of academic advancement, however, any faculty member whose profile of research productivity differs from some idealised model has to take particular care to argue for their case. The greater their difference from the norm, the more compelling their argument has to be.

Your final question had to do with your draft application for promotion, which you sent to me. I have read it through a couple of times. A lot of material in your publications list has been submitted to journals, but is not yet technically in press, in the sense that it has not been given the green light from the editor as a result of positive referees' reports. You also list your monograph as still being evaluated by the publisher, and that you plan to edit another book.

Personally, I expect the committee would consider your application this year a little premature. You have too many things in the pipeline for them to be able to get a strong sense of your peer-reviewed productivity. Were you to apply next year, firm decisions would have been reached on most of the material submitted. It may even be that reviews of your monograph will have appeared in one or more of the key journals. Until there is that independent perspective on your research and publications, the committee might find it difficult to assess the quality and extent of your contribution.

These are my observations, based on your questions and your draft promotion application. I hope they help to fill out the picture for you.

Part five

PhD STUDIES

29

Beginning a PhD

Dear Chloe-Lee,

Thank you for your inquiry about doing a higher degree by research. I note that you are deliberately choosing this option over a degree with substantial coursework, even though it involves study through a different university. There are, as you know, advantages and disadvantages to both types, which I am sure you will have already analysed and assessed.

Yes, I am keen for you to enrol in this university, and yes, I am interested in being your principal supervisor. At least, at this stage I am interested in serious exploration! But before either of us makes a formal commitment, let's see how it might work out. Only when both of us think it is the right thing should you actually enrol. Naturally, you do need to have a pretty clear understanding of what the task involves. My comments here reflect both my own attitude as a supervisor, and also the regulations common to many universities (including mine) that offer doctorates by supervised research. Note that although PhDs by research only are not uncommon, the degree rules usually allow for some preliminary coursework to be prescribed if that helps the whole enterprise along.

I want candidates to know what to expect of me, and what I normally expect of them. Research and thesis writing are serious, demanding activities, but the rewards are considerable. The prolonged and deep engagement that a thesis demands is a powerful way to develop critical and communicative skills. My expectation is that the relationship as supervisor and graduate student would be congenial and satisfying, for both the candidate and me.

The first thing would be to develop a focus for your study and to get your thoughts clarified. It is important to settle on something that gives scope for research at a level appropriate for a doctorate. It should also be something that you can manage, given your other commitments. Let me focus on the first of these.

Doing research for a doctorate in our field means knowing, theorising, reflecting and conceptualising not only about the methodology of the research but also about what the substantive issues are, how various aspects can be analysed, and how a coherent picture or explanation can be put together. This involves painstaking and prolonged thinking and reading. The best work cannot be done in a hurry. Don't despair if you think such work may be beyond you at the moment. You will already have done lots of thinking in your studies before reaching this point, and one of the purposes of doing a higher degree is to further develop your skills of conceptualising, so that ultimately you become an informed and independent thinker. We would work on that together. A thesis that consists essentially of mere description or reportage, however interesting and comprehensive, is unlikely to satisfy the criteria for scholarly work.

Don't worry either about trying to anticipate *exactly* how the research is going to finish up. True, you have to write and defend a formal proposal. If you knew now everything you are going to find out during your research, naturally you would be able to write the perfect proposal. You would also have nothing left to research because you would know all the answers.

In many disciplines, the research focus usually metamorphoses to some extent during the research anyway. This is perfectly normal. At the end of the day, you have to show evidence of sustained, in-depth research and encapsulate the results in a dissertation. But the examiners won't be sent a copy of your original proposal. Their job is to judge the quality of the research and the dissertation as they appear in the end, not to see whether the outcome agrees with an original proposal written a long time before the event.

To do a PhD by research, you have to retain an intense interest in the subject for a prolonged period, probably the equivalent of three years full time. You need to choose carefully so that you maintain momentum right to the very end. In fact, it is towards the end that keeping interested is most important. By that time, you will have spent hundreds of hours with your mind in gear on a single theme. There is some risk that you will feel sick of the sight of books and writing. The very thought of the energy you have already put in and what remains to be done may overwhelm you. Every higher degree student I have known has felt that way at times, although some students feel it more often and more keenly than others. Even when you feel completely played out, and tired of having a one-track mind, you *have* to still feel a basic interest in the topic to keep going. You have to be convinced that the study is significant and worthwhile for reasons that are above and beyond the degree you will get out of it.

I appreciate that you want the PhD to relate directly to your current job, but you need to be careful on that account. I usually warn part-time students against working too narrowly on a topic that revolves around something that could change radically, or even disappear altogether, during the time proposed for the full research project. Particular dangers are programs that are the subject of government or other public agency initiatives. A simple change in policy could leave you stranded. The last thing you want is to put a lot of time into planning and beginning research (or even worse, getting it nearly completed) only to find that, through no fault of your own, the study cannot be completed. You simply may not be able to salvage enough pieces of what you have done to put a thesis together.

On a similar note, projects in which you are involved as part of non-permanent employment, such as contract positions and secondments, are also highly risky. So are projects that involve your superior in granting you special facilities or privileges to do the degree. Clearly, these can be useful, but they depend on a particular person's occupying a position long enough for you to finish. These problems are especially acute for part-time students because the completion date cannot be guaranteed, and candidature ordinarily takes up to twice as long as for a full-time student.

It is much wiser to choose a topic that is related to some enduring and more generalisable aspect, something that will always be around, which is always problematic, and which leaves your research reasonably unaffected by changes in your employment conditions. This is not meant to deter you from relating your research to your work. It is both efficient and useful to do so. However, before you decide on a particular study, analyse what aspects of your environment are susceptible to change at short notice and take these into consideration.

I would be pleased to work with you in refining an appropriate research project. The time scale for that is not critical, but the university's resources, including borrowing rights from the library, would be available to you only after enrolment. If you put a lot of effort into exploring and developing a sense of where you want to go beforehand, your candidature will probably be shorter. What you lose on the swings you gain on the roundabouts, so don't enrol until you are ready.

Although minimum and maximum time limits for completing the PhD are specified in the rules, these limits can be varied on a case-by-case basis. Extensions beyond the usual maximum are, as it turns out, more difficult to negotiate than getting approval for an early completion.

Naturally, the student is responsible for undertaking any library searches and obtaining journal articles, including those on interlibrary loan. Advice on computer-based searches can be obtained through mini-courses sponsored by the library. Depending on the final topic we negotiate, I may have additional resources consisting of fugitive documents, conference papers and hard-to-get articles which I could lend you. In addition, I always have random jottings, various think-pieces in progress, and drafts of articles I am working on. I am prepared to share these with PhD students, on the understanding that they cannot be either referenced until I have published them or plagiarised in any way. On occasion, I will be looking for critical comments on my own work as well, and look to research students for their contributions. I will, however, take care not to steal your ideas either.

I sometimes supervise candidates on projects that are at the margins of my own academic expertise. I do this because I recognise that emerging research fields have to 'grow themselves' somewhere, and that PhD candidates are often capable of providing original insights and breaking new ground in their research. Substantive expertise is not always available for every worthwhile researchable topic. I also believe that research cloning is limiting and anti-intellectual.

In these circumstances, I can provide a testing ground for ideas and promising directions, and guidance on research methods, analytical rigour and cogent scholarly writing. But I do not undertake to read 200 disparate journal articles and ten books in a somewhat alien field to check whether the candidate's literature review is adequate. So I make it clear to such candidates, at the beginning, that they will be more or less on their own in that domain. So far, this arrangement has worked out all right.

Now back to your final query. The approval of PhD candidature is done by the university's Graduate Studies Board (GSB) on the advice of the relevant Dean, and the Higher Degrees Coordinator in the Department. Both of these rely on advice from potential supervisors. The GSB has the final say. Basically, this Board needs to be convinced that three conditions are satisfied.

Condition 1—The proposed project or investigation must be of a quality, scope and depth that:

- is appropriate to the degree (PhD) for which the candidate wishes to enrol;
- provides scope for significant theorising and theory building—that is, will lead to a dissertation that is critically analytical rather than essentially descriptive;
- makes connections with existing knowledge in the field with a view to extending it, hence the desirability for about half a dozen key references in the proposal; and
- confronts an issue or phenomenon that is important and intrinsically interesting.

Condition 2—The candidate must have sufficient knowledge, skills and determination to carry out the research. This may be judged through:

- formal qualifications, including, for entry to the PhD degree, a higher degree which involves a dissertation or substantial project report; or
- publications of an appropriate standard in scholarly outlets.

Condition 3—The university must be able to provide appropriate methodological and substantive supervision for the candidate. This includes a projection into the years of candidature, and a clear indication that supervisor and candidate will have sufficient opportunity to consult, to monitor progress, and to maintain momentum throughout the life of the project and the writing up.

The main question overall is this: is there a high probability that the candidate, under the prevailing circumstances and with the resources and supervision available, will satisfactorily complete a high-quality research project and dissertation within the specified time frame?

I look forward to your reaction to all of this. I certainly hope you want to pursue the matter further. If so, please send me a fuller outline of the type of project you are thinking about, together with a copy of a substantial piece of your own writing, such as the write-up of your masters project. I will then be able to get a feel for how we might be able to work this through.

30

Balancing competing priorities

Dear Morgan,

I am delighted to hear that you are to be offered a tenure track position, despite the standard requirement for faculty members to hold a doctoral degree before appointment. I note that the committee has stipulated that you must make substantial progress on your PhD as a condition for extending your appointment beyond the first year, and that you must complete it before tenure could be considered.

Given the circumstances, this is no doubt reasonable, but it certainly puts the pressure on you, especially when you are starting in a different institution. Besides the preparation for teaching, every university has its distinctive culture, which can take some getting used to. Fortunately, most committee memberships are voluntary, so you can at least control demands on your time from that direction. Committees will still be around later! It might not be wise to avoid committee or other administrative work altogether, though. You may well have to demonstrate an appropriate service contribution to your department or the university when your performance review comes round in a year's time.

I agree with you on the advantages of transforming your original doctoral proposal so that your research project makes a stronger connection with your teaching responsibilities. With good planning, your studies should be able to bring you to the cutting edge of your field and provide you with a research agenda for several years ahead. Although a lot of your courses will initially be at the undergraduate level, the research should stand a good chance of livening up your teaching.

When you enrolled for the PhD, you were probably supplied with some documents setting out the university's expectations with respect to being a doctoral student, the mutual responsibilities of supervisors and candidates, and maybe some other procedural things. Another set of documents could be very useful right from the early stages of your research, if you don't already have them.

When universities send copies of the dissertation to examiners, they usually send blank summary report forms for the examiners to complete. To this, they usually attach a copy of their current *Advice to Examiners of PhD Theses*, which gives details of the criteria and standards the examiners are expected to apply. These documents are not normally confidential, but for some reason they are often not made available to candidates as a matter of routine. You should have no difficulty obtaining copies from your graduate studies office on request. The documents will show how the examiners will be asked to evaluate your dissertation, which is important to know even in the early stages.

I also enclose a list of pointers that I give my own students, although they may need some modification for your particular type of project. When I am asked to examine a dissertation, I always hope for one that is interesting to read. I dread the thought of something that is long, vague or dull. The small honorarium that comes with being an examiner is hardly compensation for being bored out of your wits for days on end.

Now to your other concern. You certainly are in a difficult situation with regard to your proposed book. Having a publisher anxious to sign you up is a superb opportunity, one many academics never have. You could reasonably expect the publisher to want the manuscript finished a few months before the end of this academic year, because each book title is incorporated into a publisher's profile as part of its publicity machine. Once a contract is signed, it is binding.

You mentioned that you had a colleague in the same department who is an experienced teacher but is not in the same employment predicament as you are. Could this person take over the leading role for the book, and become first author of a joint-authored book? You may be able to come to some arrangement as to how the book might be put together, even employing, at your own expense if necessary, a research assistant to do a lot of the routine work.

After you have checked out this possibility, the obvious course of action is to explain to the publisher immediately the circumstances you are now in. If you have already signed a contract, I would not expect the publisher to be favourably disposed towards any change to the timetable.

The publisher is probably intending to have the book available for students before the beginning of the next academic year. Because the courses for which this is an appropriate text are mostly offered in first semester, missing the current deadline, and with it the full publication schedule and publicity, might put adoptions of the text back by at least one full academic year. This could provide an opportunity for a competitor's textbook to make substantial inroads into the market.

In the longer term, you may need to explore the relative emphases you should place on writing textbooks in your field and working on traditional forms of research and publication, including journal articles and scholarly monographs. You may be well positioned to make a major contribution to the curriculum in your field at a later stage, especially if there is little by way of competing books. An important consideration, obviously, is the interpretation given to scholarship in your department and university.

To create high-quality textbooks requires both scholarship into the subject matter, and scholarship in relation to the pedagogy. To date, this type of scholarship has been seriously undervalued in most university contexts, presumably because the primary audience is not literally one's academic peers. Internationally, however, there is a noticeable movement currently under way to construe 'scholarship' more in terms of the properties of the product, specifically rigour, than in terms of the publication medium. Rigour is being recognised as applicable to a wide variety of academic discourses, including books, policy analyses, technical reports and journal articles. It involves comprehensiveness, freedom from bias, evidence for conclusions and thoroughness of the logic. In terms of influencing the direction of a field, a person can sometimes achieve more by writing a high-quality, widely adopted textbook than by following a traditional research program.

DESIRABLE QUALITIES OF A DISSERTATION

- It should contain abstract thought (theorising, philosophising, wrestling with concepts, relationships and issues) and demonstrate a degree of detachment and objectivity on the part of the researcher.
- It should exhibit originality and insight, and be lean on repetitive hackwork or mere replication.
- It should be readable, coherent, and internally consistent. Lucid writing is of key importance to a dissertation. It should be well argued and clearly reasoned, but neither turgid nor apologetic.
- Possible alternative explanations, interpretations or

directions should first be anticipated or acknowledged, then examined, and finally countered or answered. This is the essence of scholarship.

- The development should be consistent with what is known, from whatever source. When the dominant thinking is challenged, the case should be made carefully and thoroughly.

- The dissertation should have its own integrity, and be largely self-authenticating, rather than being authenticated primarily through some recognised research paradigm or method. It should show evidence of self-criticism, but be neither self-deprecatory nor self-laudatory.

- If the piece of research is essentially developmental work or action research, there should be some evidence of positive impact in either clarity or action; it should not be destructive.

- The following should be played down: a long literature review, longwinded discussion on relatively minor points, and trying to keep within the constructs and language of a single discipline merely for the sake of purity.

31

Publishing during degree candidature

Dear Sam,

Having now settled on a suitable topic for your PhD thesis, your main question to me was whether it is advisable for you to publish during your candidature, before your thesis is submitted. First check the policy in your university. This will almost certainly be spelled out somewhere in the PhD degree rules. Although universities differ on this issue, they tend to be similar within a given country.

In some universities, previously published work simply cannot be incorporated into the dissertation. Other universities allow material that has already been published in, say, one or more refereed journal articles to be incorporated in whole or in part into the body of the thesis, subject to a few simple and reasonable conditions. The existence of explicit but diametrically opposite policies seems puzzling, but must be based on entirely different rationales.

Where incorporation is allowed, the rules typically state that the published material has to be made an integral part of the total document. It therefore has to be cross-referenced with other parts of the thesis where appropriate. It must flow seamlessly with the other material, the text being feathered in at both ends. The complete text must be presented in the same typeface, style and format, so that the thesis appears as a unified whole. Word processors make meeting this last requirement simple.

Apart from the technical issue of the university's policy, you will have to find out whether your principal supervisor is supportive of the idea. You will need to talk through the authorship issue as well, particularly in relation to text segments that could go into the thesis verbatim. Joint authorship with the supervisor's name first could possibly complicate things at the examination stage.

These are some advantages and disadvantages of publishing during candidature:

ADVANTAGES

- Publishing during candidature (PDC) conceptually integrates research, the thesis, and the accessibility of your work to scholars at large, which is one of the hallmarks of sound research. It links publication naturally and directly to research activity, which is the standard practice for academics.
- PDC allows you to capitalise on training for the publication phase during your enrolment. Publishing along the way enables you to be guided by your supervisor as part of your training. Once your thesis is finished and the degree awarded, it may not be quite so easy to find appropriate advice on preparing research materials for publication. Plenty of graduates never get round to publishing anything at all from their theses.
- PDC provides quality control checks on the work you are

producing, because it provides access to reviewers' comments and suggestions before a chapter is finalised. This is usually helpful to both the candidate and the supervisor.

- PDC may enable you to test the standing of your literature review and your emerging theoretical position, particularly when, as in your case, the topic is somewhat outside the mainstream of the supervisor's expertise. A heavier responsibility for the integrity of the literature review naturally falls on you. Finding a suitable journal is important. Most journals do not accept straight literature reviews, whereas a few specialise in them.

- PDC encourages an objective analysis of style and the structure of writing in a particular genre, using existing articles as models. Articles can often be more easily incorporated into the body of a thesis than can chapters of a thesis be converted into article manuscripts. The discipline of preparing a cogent manuscript can help in getting a thesis together. The thesis will be shorter, more interesting and more to the point as a result.

- One of the questions likely to be asked of your examiners is whether the thesis contains material that is publishable. If some of your work has already been published in, or is in press with, a good refereed journal, examiners are unlikely to say that it is below standard or unpublishable.

- PDC gives you a double dividend at the end. You finish with a research degree plus several publications. This can prove to be highly beneficial if you are looking for an academic post or for advancement.

DISADVANTAGES

- Writing articles can become diverting, especially if you are sidetracked from the main topic. In other words, it can work against keeping a clear focus on the research.

- Writing publishable articles requires a high standard and is quite demanding. If taken to excess, the energy consumed may prolong the length of your candidature unnecessarily.
- Finally, the articles could take off in different directions, and then become hard to relate back to the main theme of the dissertation. This has to be guarded against.

Ordinarily, I encourage the candidates whom I supervise to publish at least a proportion of their work before submitting the thesis. As I see it, my role as supervisor goes beyond that of supervision for the thesis alone. A higher degree by research is meant to be an induction into the enterprise and culture of academic research, regardless of the candidate's type of employment. It involves training another person to be a researcher in the discipline, not assisting someone to have an effective research life that lasts only as long as their degree studies. This training includes creating a climate in which curiosity, questioning and inquiry is the norm rather than the exception, and where there is considerable commitment to research as an attitude of mind. Such a climate should in turn influence a candidate's motivation. Becoming a researcher also means publishing, because publication is the natural culmination of research activity.

32

Converting your thesis into a book

Dear Richard,

I was glad to hear that your doctoral project is nearing its end and that you are in the final stages of writing your dissertation. As I suggested earlier, you should actively work on how you might publish some of the results, as your advisers are encouraging you to. Exactly how best to approach this is worth serious thought.

The primary audience for your dissertation is your committee of examiners. The audiences for publications are quite different. Also, the article, the book chapter and the monograph are distinct genres, so you need to explore the options carefully. Naturally, my comments have to be fairly general because I do not have a clear idea of how you have approached your research.

The possibilities are, as you indicate, to write some journal articles, to convert your thesis into a book more or less as a whole, or to write a series of articles first and later extend and incorporate these into a book. You asked for my view as to the most effective strategy. This is how things look from a distance. However, I wouldn't want any of my observations or suggestions to run counter to what your advisers recommend.

I will start with the task of turning the thesis into a book. Unfortunately, a thesis is almost never directly publishable as a book. If you want to write a book, I recommend that you put the thesis away altogether. Wait a while, do some homework on the potential readership of the proposed book, identify their needs, develop a book proposal, negotiate with a publisher, sign a contract, and then write the book.

The style of thesis text is typically academic: cautious, erudite, rigorous, disciplined, precise and reserved. This makes it stodgy for the ordinary reader. It comes over as ponderous, pedantic, laboured, and often downright boring or even pretentious. Although a university expects each examiner to read critically through the text, it does not follow that less dedicated readers will be prepared to pay good money for a book that is difficult to wade through.

Academic books should be clearly written and have a serious intent. But a good book will be straightforward and interesting, occasionally even adventurous and lively. I wish more theses were like that, and I am quite sure most examiners feel the same way. It is a great relief to examine a thesis that flows smoothly and is fascinating to read. So, although good 'book' text often makes for a good thesis, it mostly doesn't work the other way round.

I realise that examiners are frequently asked whether the thesis contains work that should be published. Many examiners duly respond by saying: yes, the thesis should definitely be published, ideally as a monograph. But the transformation of a thesis into a book is almost always extraordinarily difficult. Because the audience is so different, the language, style and treatment also need to be quite different. The thesis is best viewed as research work, produced under supervision, for examination by other suitably qualified researchers to accredit a candidate as a scholar or researcher.

The book is a different animal altogether. Authors (should) know a lot about their potential audience, about the content that is to go into the book and about how to communicate that content to readers. Publishers (should) know a lot about book design, book production and manufacture, and book marketing and distribution. Although an academic book may also be a work of research, it is always a joint venture between an author and a publisher, for a defined mass market, to produce a profit. Hence, if you want to write a monograph, start more or less from scratch after your thesis is completed.

When you have finished your doctorate, you will probably be among the twenty people in the world who are most knowledgeable about the particular scholarly domain you have researched. This provides you with invaluable and comprehensive background material, which is an excellent base from which to launch the writing of a book. But still consider the book as a separate project altogether. The only exception to this general rule is where a person writes up their research as a monograph in the first instance, and then submits the book and possibly related materials to a university for examination as the academic equivalent to a standard doctoral thesis. Fortunately, some universities permit this, even encourage it.

You asked me specifically about whether you should immediately publish some of your work as journal articles, in view of the fact that your whole thesis may eventually be published in book form. If your proposed book is to consist mostly, or completely, of material already published as journal articles, you could expect commercial publishers to be less than enthusiastic about the idea. Academic material that has been put into the public arena is obviously already accessible to other researchers in the field. This applies also to material 'published' on the Internet, whether connected with a thesis or not. A republication in book form would, in most situations, be a poor financial proposition. Book publishers have to make a profit to stay in business. In rare instances, though, the early publication of several significant articles that capture the interest of academic readers could well provide an important marketing tool for a book, especially if the articles strike out in a quite new direction and provoke radically different thought or even controversy.

Normally, a publisher might want to limit the amount of previously published material to 20–30 per cent of the total book content, unless the material has been substantially extended or reworked between the times of article and book publication. Obviously, though, most scholarly monographs are on themes that are consistent with the previously published research of an author.

Suppose you publish three articles over the next nine months, and that they contain a lot of ideas and theorising rather than straightforward reportage of empirical results. By the time you have a decent book proposal ready for a publisher to evaluate, your ideas on the material in those articles would almost certainly have advanced anyway. The article reviewers' comments together with the thesis examiners' comments will have helped you refine your approach to the topic. You could then incorporate these improvements into the final manuscript.

On the other hand, suppose you held off publishing journal articles because of the prospect of a full book in the future. If the book never eventuates, you may lose momentum and some good opportunities, particularly if the material is likely to date. As with many things, the benefits have to be balanced against the risks.

I understand your point that you are unable to discuss this possibility with your eventual publisher, because you don't yet have a publisher. It would still be in order for you to contact two or three potential publishers, informally at this stage, to find out what their general views would be. Choose firms that already publish titles in your area. Think through how your proposed book could complement their current list, and not compete with one of their present titles. Also know something about the books available from other publishers that yours would have to compete with. Ask to speak with the acquisitions (or commissioning) editor.

Part six

A FINAL WORD

33

Maintaining a focus on university core business

Dear Colleague,

This letter is addressed directly to you. You could have arrived at this, the last letter in the book, by having read all the other letters in order from the beginning. Or you might have skimmed the book and decided to see how it all finishes up. Maybe you just looked for the shortest letter to read first. However you arrived here, this is a restatement of what the book is about.

Many academics experience frustration and a sense of powerlessness because they do not understand the context in which they work. Becoming aware of the values and environment of higher education is the first step in organising for control of the significant aspects of career development.

This book takes a look behind the scenes in academia. It explains how the policies and procedures that are characteristic of universities work out in practice for faculty members. In particular, it explains why some activities lead to career advancement and others do not. Coordinating academic and personal priorities, and working systematically towards achieving realistic goals are necessary if academics are to develop a sense of career. Apprehension can be replaced by high levels of job satisfaction, further motivation, and an enduring sense of personal efficacy.

The agendas and influences that operate at the level of committees and senior decision makers in universities are, despite rumours, mostly sensible and rational. They are, however, seldom articulated. This is not intentional but happens by default. This book brings many of them into the open and offers practical advice on how to avoid pitfalls.

Understanding is important, but so is maintaining a clear perspective on what higher education is essentially about. The focus for us as academics is surely to facilitate the core business of a university. Real academic work consists of two primary elements:

- To teach in such a way that students' knowledge and skills bases are extended, their sensitivity to historical and contemporary issues is heightened, and students move further towards becoming independent, intrinsically motivated and self-monitoring learners.
- To extend the publicly accessible stock of knowledge through empirical, theoretical and conceptual research, scholarship and publication.

Everything else, including administration, entrepreneurship, leadership in the profession, consultancies, and service (whether to the university, to departments or to our professions) must be subservient to these two.

For me, the ideal university environment is where:

- original thought and intellectual rigour are promoted and recognised;
- intellectual freedom and diversity of opinion are steadfastly protected;

- excellence in teaching is pursued with vigour, and adequately rewarded;
- students are treated as potential colleagues;
- activities are guided by a strong sense of justice and social responsibility;
- people ask, as a matter of course, 'What are you working on?' and 'Where are you travelling?';
- most people have a sensible answer to give, and the answer changes from year to year;
- people cooperate and care for one another;
- empire building is a low priority; and
- faculty members and support staff respect each other, achieve their goals and enjoy job satisfaction.

In the end a lot of this is up to us.

Further reading

Blaxter, L., Hughes, C. and Tight, M. 1998 *The Academic Career Handbook* Open University Press, Buckingham, UK

Boice, R. 1992 *The New Faculty Member: supporting and fostering professional development* Jossey-Bass, San Francisco

Boyer, E.L. 1990 *Scholarship Reconsidered: priorities of the professoriate* Carnegie Foundation for the Advancement of Teaching, Princeton, New Jersey

Brislin, R.W. 1991 *The Art of Getting Things Done: a practical guide to the use of power* Praeger, New York

Derricourt, R. 1996 *Ideas into Books: a guide to scholarly and non-fiction publishing* Penguin, Ringwood, Victoria

Gappa, J.M. and Leslie, D.W. 1993 *The Invisible Faculty: improving the status of part-timers in higher education* Jossey-Bass, San Francisco

Luey, B. 1995 *Handbook for Academic Authors* Cambridge University Press, Cambridge

Johnson, L. 1996 *Being an Effective Academic* Oxford Centre for Staff Development, Oxford Brookes University, Oxford

Mackenzie, R.A. 1997 *Time Trap: the classic book on time*

management 3rd edn, American Management Association, New York

Pequegnat, W. and Stover, E. 1995 *How to Write a Successful Research Grant Application: a guide for social and behavioral scientists* Plenum, New York

Phillips, E.M. and Pugh, D.S. 1994 *How to Get a PhD: a handbook for students and their supervisors* Open University Press, Milton Keynes

Ramsden, P. 1992 *Learning to Teach in Higher Education* Routledge, London

Sadler, D.R. 1990 *Up the Publication Road: a guide to publishing in scholarly journals for academics, researchers and graduate students* Green Guide Series vol. 2, Higher Education Research and Development Society of Australasia, Canberra

Webb, G. 1994 *Making the Most of Appraisal: career and professional development planning for lecturers* Kogan Page, London

Index